The Global Condition

The Global Condition

CONQUERORS, CATASTROPHES, AND COMMUNITY

William H. McNeill

PRINCETON UNIVERSITY PRESS

PRINCETON, NEW JERSEY

Published by Princeton University Press, 41 William Street,
Princeton, New Jersey 08540; in the United Kingdom by
Princeton University Press, Oxford

Copyright © 1992 by Princeton University Press
All Rights Reserved

Library of Congress Cataloging-in-Publication Data

McNeill, William Hardy, 1917–
The global condition: conquerors, catastrophes, and community /
William H. McNeill.
p. cm.
"This book is comprised of The great frontier, originally published
by Princeton University Press in 1983; The human frontier
published by Princeton University Press in 1979; and 'Control and
catastrophe in human affairs,' published first in Daedalus"—
T.p. verso.
Includes index.
ISBN 0-691-08648-6 (cloth: acid-free)—ISBN 0-691-02559-2
(pbk.: acid-free)
1. Civilization—History. 2. Social history. 3. Frontier and pioneer
life—History. 4. Emigration and immigration—History. I. Title.
CB69.M335   1992
909—dc20   92-16108

First Princeton Paperback printing, 1992

Princeton University Press books are printed on acid-free paper,
and meet the guidelines for permanence and durability of the
Committee on Production Guidelines for Book Longevity of the
Council on Library Resources

1 3 5 7 9 10 8 6 4 2
1 3 5 7 9 10 8 6 4 2
(pbk.)

Printed in the United States of America

Table of Contents

Preface   *vii*

[v]

Preface

ENDOWED LECTURESHIPS require universities to find someone to say something in public at a date set only a few months in advance. The essays assembled in this book all derive from this circumstance. The first two, entitled "The Human Condition," were delivered as Bland-Lee lectures at Clark University in 1979. The two essays on "The Great Frontier" were Edmondson lectures at Baylor University in 1982. And the last of them, "Control and Catastrophe in Human Affairs," originated as the Henry Stafford Little lecture delivered at Princeton University in 1986.

The texts have been minimally revised for publication, partly because I feel that what purports to be a lecture ought to be faithful to the occasion, and partly because I like to start a new inquiry as soon as a given enterprise has arrived at its appointed end. Perhaps this preserves a certain freshness; it certainly means that the topics dealt with in these pages are treated hastily, with many ramifications left unexplored. Indeed, their sketchy nature is what binds them together, for these lectures are all part of an effort to express more adequately an emerging and still imperfect notion of what really matters in human history.

The central issue, it seems to me, is how historians ought to address the relationship between conscious *purposes*, which once were the sole concern of most historians, and *processes* that transcend human intentions, and may or may not be apparent to those affected by them. The relation of purpose to process has always been puzzling to ordinary people, for the best laid plans and most carefully prepared actions of which we are capable regularly produce unforeseen consequences—sometimes disastrous, sometimes indifferent, and sometimes serendipitous.

We all inherit two very powerful answers to the persistent discrepancy between expectation and actual experience. Providence, as set forth in the Bible, explains that human purposes get twisted and altered in application because they must either collaborate or collide with God's omnipotent will. Alternatively, classical Greek writers—dramatists and historians as well as philosophers—suggested that gods as well as men were subject to fate, which was sometimes personified as the Three Fates, and sometimes conceived as ineluctable Necessity—a sort of natural law, or at least law-like in its workings. If law-like, perhaps human minds could decipher its principles, and this possibility entranced the Athenian tragedians as well as Herodotus and Thucydides. Yet the effort to anatomize fate by looking for acts of hubris and consequent disaster, though it created two very powerful historical narratives, could not explain the politics of the Hellenistic age; and the rise of Rome, when it occurred, violated all the rules of moderation inasmuch as Roman hubris went unpunished for centuries. When at length the Roman empire began to decay, divine Providence, as shaped within the Judeo-Christian heritage, took over as the only adequate explanation of what happened in history.

Until Newton came along with a new view of celestial and terrestrial motion it seemed self-evident to Europeans that human purposes were only a subordinate factor in determining what happened in history, since God used human initiatives to fulfil His own inscrutable purposes. But when the mathematical elegance of Newton's world machine had been published to the world, divine intervention in the natural world began to seem like a desecration. Moreover, if God refrained from working miracles out of respect for the laws of motion that He had established for the cosmos, there ought also to be laws governing human affairs. The question of how purpose and process combine to make history was thereby reopened, and the puzzle remains unresolved to this day.

In course of the nineteenth century, the ambition to achieve a science of society analogous to the sciences of physics and astronomy resulted in the emergence of sociology. By the end of the century, it became institutionalized as an academic pursuit, even though the hoped-for laws of human society had yet to be discovered. Historians followed a different path, largely because the study of history became an academic subject (at least in Germany) early in the nineteenth century at a time when reaction against the godlessness of the French revolution was in full force. Hence Ranke, and nearly all the other academic pioneers of "scientific" history, affirmed that God presided over history in some ultimate sense, even though the inscrutability of His purposes meant that specific evidence of divine intervention could not be pinned down. Instead of speculating on the role of Providence in human affairs, they preferred to ask questions susceptible to definitive, "scientific," answers. What really happened might, they hoped, be teased from written records by reading all available sources, comparing them carefully, and combing out anything contrary to human or natural probability as they understood it.

Much was in fact achieved by these methods. A detailed, primarily political, narrative of European history in medieval and early modern times emerged from German seminars, and shortly before the close of the nineteenth century the technique was transferred to the United States and applied to American as well as to European history. This was the scholarly tradition that my teachers sought to transmit to me in the 1930s. I was not perfectly satisfied by their ideas and methods at the time, and have subsequently explored some of the aspects of human affairs that were left out or underemphasized by my predecessors.

First of all, and most conspicuously, this meant broadening the scope of historical study to embrace the four-fifths of humanity that had been tacitly excluded from attention by my teachers, for whom only European and American history mattered. The shift from a Eurocentric to a global vision of the human past is still in process, but seems to be gaining ground rather rapidly in our schools, with the help of a few professional historians and textbook writers who have provided diverse models of how the entirety of the human adventure on earth may be organized and presented to the young.

It is really quite obvious that all human societies deserve a place in our historical consciousness, but it is far more difficult to decide what really matters. History as a course of study cannot be exhaustive: too much is knowable. What should be left out to make the past intelligible?

An easy answer is to select data from the past to enhance group consciousness. This is in fact what most historians have done, both before and after the dawn of "scientific" history in German universities. National histories were the great achievement of the first generations of professional academic historians; more recently the consciousness of subnational (and often aggrieved) groups has been the preferred focus. But world historians, by definition, cannot get far by cultivating the self-consciousness of any existing human group.

Consciousness of the human species as a whole is potential rather than actual. But just as most of the nations of the earth were created by political events, and then, with the help of historians, achieved a common consciousness, so, it seems to me, real human consciousness can only be expected to arise after political and economic processes have created such a tight-knit human community that every people and polity is forced to recognize its subordination to and participation in a global system. We are not far short of that condition in the last decade of the twentieth century, and world historians, if they are able to construct plausible accounts of how that circumstance arose across the centuries, can perhaps do for humanity as a whole what national historians did for emerging nations in the nineteenth and twentieth centuries, and what more specialized historians have done with conspicuous success for a number of aggrieved subnational groups since World War II.

If so, it seems to me also obvious that world historians will have to address the puzzle of purpose and process that was dismissed by our predecessors as beyond their proper concern. The reason for this is that the important changes of world history flowed across political boundaries and were not ordinarily under anyone's deliberate control. This brings the persistent discrepancy between purpose and process to the fore. As long as the backbone of history was political narrative (as was the case for national historians), discrepancies between purpose and what actually happened could ordinarily be attributed to the clash of wills among rivals for political power, both domestic and foreign. This allowed historians to leave God and other ultimate questions out of their accounts. They could stay comfortably close to what their sources had to say about things said and done, and dismiss consideration of factors in the situation of which contemporaries were not aware.

But when historians seek to address the history of the whole world, a narrative centered on the words and deeds of governing elites does not make sense. Elite consciousness, even in the largest empires of the past, remained local, yet there were connections that linked states and peoples together into what may be called a world system. By this I mean a diverse assemblage of human societies that were sufficiently in contact with one another for ideas, goods, infections, crops, and techniques to circulate among them. Before sailors learned to cross the world's oceans, separate world systems developed around centers of high skills in several parts of the world; as time went on the Eurasian world system outgrew all the rest.

Since 1500, as a result, what was originally a Eurasian system of intercommunicating societies has become genuinely global. Accordingly, transcultural or world history, which ordinarily escaped the notice of scribes and officials in the deeper past, has become more and more conspicuous. So much is this so that writing national history without attention to global entanglements is getting to be impossible. But if one seeks to discern the historic origin and development of the newly apparent world system, reliance on collating, comparing, and criticizing written documents that happen to have survived in accessible archives is no longer a very satisfactory way to proceed. Historians need instead to look for evidences of large-scale, long-range processes that figured marginally if at all in official documents, yet occasionally altered conditions of human life, and sometimes did so drastically.

Transport and communication networks obviously affected the way novelties of every kind spread within world systems of the past, and breakthroughs in transport, whenever they took place, changed the pattern of encounters across cultural and political boundaries. Diffusion (and adaptation) of tools, art forms, and other material technologies often left tangible traces that can be discovered by historians sensitive to such matters. In addition, the penetration of disease germs and of other organisms into new environments affected human life in ways that sometimes became critically important. The ravages of imported European and African diseases among native American peoples is the most obvious example of what could happen when new transport linkages were established. More recently, the arrival in Europe of a fungus that invaded and killed the leaves of potato plants in the 1840s provoked the Irish famine of 1845-1846, with far-reaching consequences for British, American, and indeed world history.

How can such complexity become comprehensible? The essays gathered here explore this problem in a very preliminary and imperfect fashion, for the plain fact is that I have not worked out an adequate answer to the puzzle of how things actually happen, whether on a global or on a more local scale. I do not expect to be able to do so, and in light of contemporary understandings of chaotic processes in such domains as weather and (perhaps also) the birth and death of stars, I do not expect anyone will ever achieve a predictive science of human society. But that does not mean that we cannot try to understand more about the processes within which human purposes are embedded.

In particular, I have become far more aware since 1963, when my major effort at a history of the world was first published, that what happens among humankind is embedded within events affecting the biosphere as a whole. This was the burden of my lectures at Clark: to sketch an ecological and historical vision of the human condition, as the subtitle states. I have also become more acutely aware of the role of demographic surges and crashes in human affairs. This gave shape to my lectures on the Great Frontier, for I claim that the diverse societies that arose in frontier regions were a response to the juxtaposition of surging populations in the disease-experienced portions of the globe with the catastrophic decay of previously isolated populations due to their novel exposure to disease.

The drastic upheaval arising from the interaction of biological and cultural encounters along the Great Frontier of modern times may in turn be conceived as a recent and particularly dramatic example of more general patterns of human experience, and this is the theme of the final essay of this collection. For, as

I say towards the close of that lecture, I have come to the conclusion that human affairs are embedded within a hierarchy of equilibria systems: physico-chemical, biological, and semiotic. A characteristic of this hierarchy is that changes at one level intrude upon and alter the balances of the others, sometimes in truly surprising fashions. The development of life on earth, for instance, is now believed to have changed the chemical character of the atmosphere, and human beings routinely alter the biological and physico-chemical balances around us by using symbols to organize common action among large numbers of persons.

In such an equilibrium system, human purposes and plans are both critical and extraordinarily fragile. They are critical because human initiatives, based on conscious purposes and plans, are the most changeable element in the system as a whole. They persistently introduce turbulence, keeping semiotic, biological, and physico-chemical equilibria continually in upheaval. Yet at the same time, human purposes are extraordinarily fragile because they never take full account of the circumstances upon which they impinge, and every so often act as triggers, provoking results that were not imagined by those who precipitated them. It follows, I think, that the more skillful human beings become at making over natural balances to suit themselves, the greater the potential for catastrophe.

Such a conclusion is not much use in trying to decipher the way history actually happened. It is worth asserting, all the same, as a reminder of how ignorant we still are about the consequences of our actions. The more we know and try to understand, the more we become aware of the uncertainty and open-endedness of human history. We change behavior constantly, without foreseeing the results accurately. We remain submerged in a vast evolutionary process that began with the Big Bang (probably) and is heading towards an unknown future—

a system in which matter and energy evolve, stars form and break apart, the solar system took form and will eventually collapse (but not before life does), and human societies emerged on planet Earth, beginning an evolution whose end is not yet in sight. And because we use words and symbols to make sense of all around us, the odd and remarkable result is that we know (or think we know) a great deal about how things got to be the way they are—including the present state of humanity and its innumerable subgroupings.

From such an angle of vision, history has become a truly imperial discipline, engulfing all others, and presenting historians with a task of digesting and ordering a range of data far greater than satisfied our predecessors, for whom constructing national histories on the basis of archival sources was the limit of their ambition. No one is ever likely to put all knowledge together in a way that will command the assent of all reasonable persons, yet trying to understand is irresistible. That is how human minds treat the world around them—making sense out of it by inventing explanations, generalizing actual experience, and projecting their ideas (expressed of course in symbols) upon the universe at large.

Human beings have always done so. My reflections, speculations, and investigations are only a recent, idiosyncratic example of a universal human habit. I invite readers to construct a historical worldview of their own by picking and choosing from everything they know, rejecting and altering what I have to say to suit themselves. Such an enterprise speaks to one of our deepest impulses—to understand the world around us by connecting everyday details with what really matters.

27 November 1991

PART I

The Great Frontier

FREEDOM AND HIERARCHY
IN MODERN TIMES

Acknowledgments

THESE ESSAYS were originally prepared for delivery at Baylor University, March 31–April 1, 1982, as the fourth Charles Edmondson Historical Lectures. Professor Rufus B. Spain arranged the invitation and chose the topic from among several I suggested; thus he can justly claim part credit for what follows.

Since that time, my colleagues at the University of Chicago—John Coatsworth, David Galenson, Friedrich Katz, and Arthur Mann—improved the text by making suggestions and correcting mistakes in my first formulation. Members of my class in "Human Ecology since 1750," Autumn 1982, also read the manuscript and drew my attention to a few passages needing emendation. Finally, my wife and daughter combed out snarls in my prose with the patient diligence their forebears on the frontier reserved for untangling wool.

For this help, and for the sympathetic enthusiasm of Edward Tenner of Princeton University Press, I am truly grateful.

Chicago   William H. McNeill
January 1983

LECTURE I: TO 1750

IN THE LATTER part of the nineteenth century, east coast city dwellers in the United States had difficulty repressing a sense of their own persistent cultural inferiority vis-à-vis London and Paris. At the same time a great many old-stock Americans were dismayed by the stream of immigrants coming to these shores whose diversity called the future cohesion of the Republic into question almost as seriously as the issue of slavery had done in the decades before the Civil War. In such a climate of opinion, the unabashed provinciality of Frederick Jackson Turner's (1861-1932) paper "The Significance of the Frontier in American History," delivered at a meeting of the newly founded American Historical Association in connection with the World Columbian Exposition in Chicago (1892), began within less than a decade to resound like a trumpet call, though whether it signalled advance or retreat remained profoundly ambiguous.

On the one hand, if Turner were to be believed, effete easterners need not have worried about lagging behind European civilization. Instead, a new nation, with a sturdy character of its own, had already formed under western skies, since "the advance of the frontier has meant a steady movement away from the influence of Europe, a steady growth of independence along American lines."[1] National unity and national identity were safe and sound too, because "In the crucible of the frontier the immigrants were Americanized, liberated and fused into a mixed race, English neither in nationality nor characteristics."[2] Persistent cultural difference from Europe was therefore evidence not of inferiority, but of a unique and indigenous response to free land and other freedoms of the

[5]

frontier, since it is "to the frontier that the American intellect owes its striking characteristics."[3]

On the other hand, as Turner was careful to remark in both his first and last sentences, the Bureau of the Census had officially declared the frontier extinct in 1890. What did that portend for the future of American civilization? Might not the frontier-generated uniqueness of the United States decay as rapidly as it had arisen? In Turner's own words: "He would be a rash prophet who should assert that the expansive character of American life has now entirely ceased. . . . But never again will such gifts of free land offer themselves."[4]

The frontier thesis therefore appealed to optimists and pessimists, westerners and easterners alike. The extraordinary attention Turner's idea continues to receive attests the breadth of its resonance within our society.[5]

Some two generations later, Walter Webb (1888-1963) extended Turner's thesis beyond American borders by propounding the idea of a Great Frontier extending all the way around the globe.[6] Webb argued that this Great Frontier had the effect of bringing windfall profits into the European metropolis, and these profits in turn sustained a prolonged era of economic expansion from 1500 onward. Windfalls came in the form of free land for European settlers in Asia, Africa, and Australia as well as in North and South America, and also as a vast treasure trove of easily exploited gold and silver. But after about 1900 frontier windfalls became a thing of the past. The depression of the 1930s, in the midst of which Webb conceived his book, therefore registered the end of the frontier-based era of easy times not just in American but also in world history. In Webb's hands the frontier thesis thus became unambiguously pessimistic as to the future. Partly for that reason, perhaps, his idea has been far less influential than

Turner's, and, except in Texas,[7] was soon rejected by historians and forgotten by the public.

There were compelling reasons for this rejection. World War II and the thirty-year boom that followed certainly seemed to invalidate Webb's gloomy economic prophecies. In addition, after World War II American historians decided that the expansion of Europe was no longer a respectable field of academic endeavor. Instead, it became fashionable to assist the peoples of Asia and Africa in throwing off European imperialism by writing their histories for them.[8] Accordingly, Webb's synoptic vision met short shrift. Experts found that frontiers in Australia, South Africa, and Latin America were not the same as the frontier in North America, where the behavior of French and English pioneers also differed. Meanwhile, Europe itself faded from historians' purview. National, regional, and thematically specialized research took pride of place as professors of European history at American colleges and universities responded to the breakup of European world power and to cheaper transatlantic air fares by trying to rival European scholars at their own game of improving accuracy by exhausting the archives.

There was, however, an oddly isolated intellectual countercurrent in the postwar American academic scene. It stemmed from an effort, funded and sponsored by the Social Science Research Council, to transcend the traditional fragmentation of social studies as embodied in university departments by bringing the entire spectrum of humanistic and social science sensibilities to bear upon the study of a particular human society or some geographical region. Cross disciplinary area studies therefore nurtured large views without ever quite achieving academic respectability.

This was the situation that stimulated Louis Hartz to draw on his American studies background at Harvard to write a provocative book titled *Founding of New Societies: Studies in the History of the United States, Latin America, South Africa, Canada, and Australia* (New York, 1969). Hartz and his associates (for he farmed out detailed analysis of Latin America, South Africa, Canada, and Australia to like-thinking colleagues) found a meaningful pattern in the very diversity of frontier experiences. The local differences that, according to others, discredited Webb's synthetic idea made sense to Hartz because he saw in each overseas transplant a mere fragment of the original complexity of European class structures. Each such segment, torn from its original context, having rooted itself on new ground, subsequently evolved according to a logical dynamic of its own, and departed from the European norm and from other patterns of frontier development because of the fragmentary, lopsided character of the initial transfers.

Such a view affirmed the central importance of the European heritage in determining subsequent social and cultural development. Simultaneously, it emphasized deficiencies in what had been transferred to new ground. Hartz's vision of American culture and society therefore implied, without explicitly affirming, an enduring inferiority of the American "fragment" when compared to the full complexity of the European matrix whence it had been excised. In so characterizing American life he gave fresh voice to cultivated easterners' longstanding alienation from the crudity of the backwoods that Turner and Webb had deemed worthy of celebration. Terms of debate altered: witness the quasi-Marxist epithets "feudal," "bourgeois," and "radical" that Hartz used to characterize his new societies. But the debate continued to pit the effete east against the brash west as before.

Hartz's portrait of frontier societies seems to me therefore quite as provincial as Turner's and just as much in need of refurbishing. And refurbish we must if the history of the United

States, taken as a whole, is to become really intelligible once again. For if we want to make sense of all the local, ethnic, and thematic dimensions of the American past, to which professional historians have devoted their principal efforts of late, we very much need a framework into which the entire national experience in all its facets will somehow fit. Otherwise more and more facts, however well attested in the sources, become a burden on the memory, and the study of our history runs the risk of turning into mere antiquarianism.

The trouble is that the over-optimistic view of earlier generations who saw the meaning of American history in material progress, guaranteed and sustained by liberty as experienced on the frontier and codified into the Constitution, now seems inadequate. Too many people were left out: blacks, women, ethnics.

Class consciousness, even in Louis Hartz's modulated form, turned out to be an entirely inadequate substitute. This was not solely because, as the official ideology of an unfriendly power, Marxism carried a taint of treason in post-World War II United States. The real deficiency of Marxist views was that class differences did not accurately coincide with the rather more acute ethnic, religious, and racial fissures in American society. Moreover, a vision emphasizing class struggle disrupted nationwide unity and fellow feeling and exacerbated frictions with other human beings who were uncomfortably close at hand. Accordingly, Marxist versions of United States history have remained sectarian, quite incapable of remedying the inadequacies of the older, evangelical and liberal, vision of our past.

Professional response among historians was to concentrate on detail, hoping that from more and more facts a better portrait of the whole would somehow emerge, quite of its own accord. But histories of all the various groupings into which

Americans have consciously divided themselves, and might be divided by historians in retrospect, do not add up to a history of the nation as a whole any more than separate histories of each county in each state, if set side by side on library shelves, would provide a substitute for a history of the United States. Fragmented vision and close attention to detail do not necessarily improve accuracy. Focusing on separate trees may obscure the forest; preoccupation with an infinitude of differing leaves may allow the tree itself to disappear from view. Every increase in historical detail, in other words, risks losing sight of larger patterns which may be more important for public action and understanding than anything segmented sub-histories can discover.

The opposite extreme of looking at the history of this nation as part of a far larger process of European expansion may seem calculated to deprive the United States of its uniqueness. But if appropriately modulated to recognize both differences and uniformities, it seems to me that this perspective provides a far more adequate and comprehensive vision of our past than anything older nationalistic histories of liberty and prosperity had to offer. It puts the United States back into the world as one of a family of peoples and nations similarly situated with respect to the old centers of European civilization. Moreover, by taking seriously the Great Frontier phenomenon of modern times, we will find plenty of room for the downtrodden and poor as well as for the rich and successful, and thus avoid one of the main reproaches leveled against the liberal, establishmentarian version of the American past.

Here lay Webb's great achievement. He offered an appropriate framework for reappraising the history of this country by recognizing that our past was part of a global process of civilizational expansion. Progress and liberty, so dear to our forebears, played a part in the process; but so did their op-posites—slavery and the destruction of all those non-European cultures and societies that got in the way. By accepting such a framework, therefore, the successes *and* the failures can all find appropriate scope in our history if we are wise and sensitive enough to see the persistent double-edgedness of change—destroying *and* preserving, denying *and* affirming established values of human life, everywhere and all the time.

Foolhardy though it may be, this is what I propose to undertake in these lectures. Foolhardy—but not impossible: for what matters is perspective and proportion, not detail.

. . .

WEBB'S Great Frontier, like Turner's, was a region where men with skills derived from Europe met Amerindians and other "savage" peoples who were quite unable to resist the advances of white settlers. The "free land" that white men appropriated was land once used by others. The expansion of one society occurred only at the cost of another's destruction. As such, the American frontier was merely an extreme case of contact and collision between societies at different levels of skill—a pattern that runs throughout recorded history, and constitutes one of the main themes of the human past.

When peoples of approximately equal levels of skill, numbers, and organization meet on a frontier, drastic geographical displacements are unlikely. Minor fluctuations in the demarcation zone can be expected, with fluctuations in the incidence of victory and defeat. But as long as the parties remain nearly equal, no very drastic change can, by definition, occur. Minor borrowing back and forth is to be expected. Techniques and ideas that for some reason have novelty value may pass from one society to its neighbor. But it is only when inherited institutions on one side of the demarcation line cease to work well that more fundamental change becomes in the least likely, for most human beings most of the time prefer the safe and familiar to anything new. When, however, institutional decay weakens effective resistance to alien pressure, world-historical changes may ensue. Civilizational benchmarks like those signalized by Alexander's conquests of western Asia and Egypt, the Germanic invasions of the Roman empire, or the Moslem conquests of the Middle East and northern Africa record these extraordinary shifts.

Such events are rare and exceptional inasmuch as they fall outside the range of everyday encounters. An ordinary and therefore more important frontier phenomenon arose whenever one society abutted upon another that was somewhat less or more skilled. When the skill-short participant in such an encounter became aware of the difference, efforts to borrow skills needed to catch up and overtake the stronger neighbor were likely to follow. Alternatively, the weaker party might undertake measures to strengthen home defenses against an alien way of life that seemed to threaten something precious in the local cultural heritage. Far-ranging, deep-going social transformations may be triggered by either reaction.

This, indeed, seems to me to be the principal drive wheel of historic change. Encounters with strangers whose ways were different, and often threatening as well, were in all probability the main factor provoking and propagating inventions from the most ancient times to the present. And from the time when crossroads societies first achieved skills distinctly superior to those of their neighbors, i.e., since civilization first appeared on this earth, incessant interaction between more skilled and less skilled peoples has been in train. The upshot, despite numerous back-eddies and local breakdowns of civilized complexity, has been an ineluctable expansion of the portions of the globe subjected to or incorporated within civilized social structures.

Inside any given civilization an analogous interaction may

also be detected between center and periphery, capital and provinces, upper and lower classes. For civilized societies were created and are sustained by dint of occupational differentiation and specialization. Varying skills and conflicting interests therefore divide civilized communities against themselves. Such internal frictions and differentiation merge with the polarity between civilized and fringe "barbarian" communities by almost imperceptible degrees, for civilizational boundaries are always imprecise.

My proposition boils down to the assertion that cultural differentiation generated historical change, whether within a civilized society, or across its borders. Climatic and other limits of course checked the interactive process. Agricultural skills could not readily be transferred to desert land. Disease barriers were also often important in checking expansion of dense forms of human settlement onto new ground. Protection costs against hostile military harassment were sometimes too high for cultivators to sustain on ground otherwise propitious for them. For all these reasons, the cultural landscape of the earth never approached uniformity, even though the high skills initially confined to a few civilized centers did tend to spread to new places as the generations succeeded one another.[9]

As long as patterns of transport and communication changed slowly, cultural interaction proceeded century after century without generating a frontier of the sort Turner and Webb celebrated. Differences between adjacent peoples were kept within relatively modest bounds because new skills diffused in short bursts across limited distances and among peoples of nearly equivalent levels of knowledge and organization. A few conspicuous gaps, like that between steppe nomads and settled agriculturalists, became chronic, based, as they were, on contrasting human adaptations to enduring geographical diversity.

[13]

The gap between pastoral and agricultural societies long remained critically important in the Old World. This was because important zones where nomads penetrated tilled land existed across a broad region of the eastern hemisphere: along the edges of the African savanna, and across the borders of the even more extensive steppe and desert lands of Eurasia. From the time when pastoral nomads first learned to shoot arrows from horseback, about 800 B.C., until the fourteenth century A.D., military advantage consistently rested with the peoples of the desert and steppe who moved faster, and could therefore concentrate superior force at a given locality almost at will. The political history of civilized Eurasia and of Africa, in fact, consists largely of intermittent conquest by invaders from the grasslands, punctuated by recurrent rebellions of agricultural populations against subjugation to the heirs of such conquerors. Only at the two extremes of the Old World, in Japan and western Europe, were these rhythms of alternating nomad conquest and agricultural revolt too weak to matter very much.[10]

So far as I can tell, an "open" frontier of the kind that developed in North and South America, Australia, and South Africa after 1500 never arose in earlier times. Perhaps when neolithic farming folk first spread their fields across Eurasia, penetrating forests where hunting bands had previously roamed, something faintly analogous to the modern frontier arose. But that happened long before the dawn of recorded history, and the archaeological record does not show whether the advance of agriculture involved wholesale displacement of populations, as on the American frontier, or whether hunters already on the ground simply learned from neighbors how to supplement their kill by making fields and raising crops. Both processes presumably were at work, in what proportion no one can tell.

The closest analogue to the modern frontier phenomenon

in the deeper past seems to be the expansion of Chinese society southward from its original home in the Yellow River valley. Chinese colonization started before 800 B.C., and continued sporadically to the present. It was therefore a relatively slow, massive, and sustained process, involving the wholesale remodelling of natural landscapes. The Chinese built rice paddies as they advanced, leveling each field precisely, and arranging for suitable inflow of water so as to keep the surface submerged during the growing season. On most larger streams, effective water management required canal construction, diking, and other improvements to natural water courses. The settlers thereby created a transport network that tied China's expanding body politic together as effectively—perhaps, indeed, more effectively—than did the Confucian bureaucracy that oversaw the whole effort.

Like the ponderous, slow-moving Pleistocene ice sheets, whose scouring action transformed the landscape of northern Eurasia and much of North America, the expanding human mass of Chinese settlers engulfed earlier inhabitants of the Yangtze valley and regions farther south, incorporating them into the Chinese world. Human numbers and the enormous investment of labor, skill, and organization involved in making the natural landscape over into paddy fields surrounded and then submerged earlier occupants. Military action played very little part in the process. What mattered were the picks, shovels, and hoes of countless millions of pioneers, laboring persistently year after year after year, under the direction of government officials.[11]

Perhaps Andean civilization expanded in pre-Columbian times in a similar fashion. Certainly the abandoned terraces that still cling to Peruvian mountainsides constitute an impressive monument to past human effort. The taming of other regions to agriculture must also have involved prolonged, anonymous human labor on a massive scale. But until modern times, no-where, so far as I know, did the process involve ingestion of one population by another on anything approaching the scale that occurred across the Chinese southern frontier. That was because the Chinese had skills as farmers and water engineers that contiguous peoples lacked, and were ready to submit to a labor discipline that others resisted. China's historic magnitude, cohesion, and population density resulted—traits quite unparalleled elsewhere.[12]

But China's slow-moving frontier paled before the extraordinary circumstances that confronted Europeans after 1500. For the overseas expansion that followed hard on the heels of European voyages of discovery was matched by a landward expansion of almost comparable significance. European settlers began to drift into the Ukraine and adjacent areas of the western steppe in the sixteenth century, finding empty or almost empty grasslands awaiting them. This was because older nomad populations had shrunk back, retreating in all likelihood from exposure to bubonic plague, which had become endemic among the burrowing rodents of the western steppe in the fourteenth century.[13] In the course of the next two hundred years, the western steppe was firmly incorporated into European agricultural society by Slavic and Rumanian pioneers who did the work, acting, for the most part, under the legal control of noble estate owners and entrepreneurs, often of a different nationality.

The scope of this "eastward movement" bears comparison with the more familiar westward movement across North America. Expansion of agriculture into the drier and more easterly portions of the steppe continued sporadically throughout the nineteenth and into the twentieth centuries. The latest episode came in the 1950s, when the Russians plowed up millions of acres of marginal steppe lands in Kazakhstan in order to remedy the persistent grain shortages that had long plagued their planning.

Europe's landward frontier extended northward through forested land as well. There, agriculture was seldom practicable but fur-bearing animals abounded. Medieval fur traders, operating from such northern cities as Novgorod, successfully solved the problems of long-distance travel and survival in the Arctic and sub-Arctic regions of northern Russia. Once across the Urals (by 1580), therefore, Russian fur traders could move from one Siberian river system to another by making a series of easy portages. This they already knew how to do. Consequently, explorers reached Okhotsk on the Pacific coast as early as 1637. A vast land, thinly populated by weakly organized hunters and gatherers, thus came under Russian control. A little later, but in almost the same fashion, other fur traders, operating from Montreal (after 1642) and from the shores of Hudson Bay (after 1670) extended their control over the Canadian Arctic. As is well known, the rival fur-trading empires met in the 1780s when Russian pioneers who had crossed to Alaska collided with British, American, and Spanish claimants to the Pacific coastlands of North America.[14]

Because of our national origins, we in this country are far more conscious of the overseas dimension of Europe's expansion. Nor is this merely the result of myopic local perspective. European ships did in fact inaugurate more drastic new encounters after 1500 than anything happening overland within Eurasia. This justifies us in giving pride of place to European frontiers overseas, for nothing in earlier ages can quite compare with the revolution in older human balances inaugurated by those famous voyages—Columbus to Magellan, 1492-1521—so remarkably concentrated into a single generation.

Thereafter, Europeans commanding skills accumulated across millennia of civilized history found themselves face to face with previously isolated and therefore low-skilled peoples in many parts of the earth. In Australia, for example, to cite the most extreme case, European intruders met aborigines whose way of life, as attested archaeologically, seems to have altered very little after their initial penetration of the continent thousands of years before. Even in the New World, where far more accomplished Amerindian societies, like those of Mexico and Peru, came up against Spanish conquistadors, they, too, proved quite unable to resist the newcomers. Numbers were all on the side of the Amerindians at first. Spanish skills and organization, though undoubtedly superior, were not so enormously above the levels attained by the Aztecs and Incas as to compensate for the small numbers of those who followed Cortez and Pizarro, whether at the time of their conquests, or subsequently. But European epidemiological superiority was indubitable and decisive. Inherited and acquired immunities to a formidable array of lethal infections allowed Europeans to survive in the presence of killers such as smallpox, measles, flu, tuberculosis, diphtheria, and others, whereas the inexperienced Amerindians proved vulnerable to wholesale destruction on first encountering these infections.[15]

Lethal diseases from Europe and, ere long, also from Africa (yellow fever and malaria in particular) demoralized survivors and paralyzed Amerindian efforts to mount resistance against European political and cultural domination. In many places, depopulation became almost total, leaving unoccupied land for European settlers to appropriate freely. Thus the "empty" frontier Turner spoke of arose from the destruction of Amerindian populations by infections imported from the Old World, sporadically reinforced by resort to armed force. Similar epidemiological disasters afflicted other formerly isolated inhabitants of Oceania, South Africa, and, indeed, wherever a disease-inexperienced population encountered disease-resistant pioneers and explorers. Siberian hunters and trappers met the same fate when Russian fur traders initiated contacts with them, for example; and Eskimos in the Canadian Arctic were experiencing a parallel catastrophe as recently as the 1940s.[16]

The combination of epidemiological superiority with a greater or lesser superiority of skills on the part of intrusive Europeans was what gave the Great Frontier its unique character.

Nevertheless, it is worth emphasizing that not all the uncivilized parts of the earth were hospitable to European penetration. Until about 1850, tropical Africa was very effectively guarded by a formidable array of local diseases which mowed down European and Asian intruders as ruthlessly as European diseases mowed down previously isolated people of the temperate zones. African peoples of the rain forest and savanna south of the Sahara therefore remained in undisturbed possession of their ancestral lands. The slave trade soon assumed hitherto unexampled scale among them, supplying labor to European-managed plantations in the New World and to Moslem households and plantations in the Old in approximately equal numbers.[17] Slave raiding undoubtedly altered older patterns of human life in Africa in far-reaching ways. Simultaneously, the spread of maize and of other new crops from America began to provide a far more productive basis for African agriculture. Changes must have been drastic under these circumstances. But Africa did *not* become a theater for European frontier expansion save for a small area in the extreme south, where a cooler, drier climate prevented tropical diseases from spreading.

Before 1750, therefore, the steppe and forest zones of Eurasia, together with North and South America, constituted the principal regions where frontier encounters assumed the extraordinary form familiar to us from our own national history. This was where Europeans could and did begin to occupy land emptied, or almost emptied, of older inhabitants by the catastrophic juxtaposition of disease-experienced civilized populations with epidemiologically and culturally[18] vulnerable natives. Nothing comparable had ever happened before. European expansion therefore assumed unparalleled proportions. The process gave birth to the two politically dominant states of our own time, the USSR and the USA, one east and the other west of the older centers of European civilization. Brazil and the diverse states of Spanish America are likewise heirs of this frontier. So is South Africa; but the European encroachment on Australia, New Zealand, and other Pacific islands did not begin until after the middle of the eighteenth century and so does not yet enter our purview.

The most salient characteristic of the Great Frontier created by the combined ravages of civilized diseases, alcohol, and firearms on indigenous populations was that human numbers were or soon became scant in the contact zone. Anyone who wished to exploit the land agriculturally or sought to mine precious metals or extract other raw materials faced a problem of finding an adequate labor force to do the necessary work. Shortage of manpower meant that European skills and knowledge could not readily be brought to bear in frontier lands, no matter how richly they were endowed.

Carrying Europeans across the seas to remedy this situation was expensive. Relatively few ever made the crossing before the 1840s, when steamships began to cheapen passage and to enlarge passenger carrying capacity. Estimates of transatlantic migration are very inexact, since early records of voyages across the ocean are spotty at best and seldom include passenger lists. A recent guess set the total of British immigrants to North America before 1780 at 750,000 and of French to Canada at only 10,000.[19] Further south no careful calculation of any general total of European immigration exists, though what scraps of evidence there are suggest that something like a million persons crossed the ocean to take up residence in the Caribbean and Latin America before 1800.[20]

Spaniards did, of course, employ Amerindians in the mines and for innumerable building projects and other enterprises in the first rush of their conquest. But the extreme vulnerability of such a labor force to epidemic disease led to heavy loss of life and soon made recruitment difficult. In most islands of the Caribbean the Amerindian population died out completely. Amerindians also disappeared almost totally from the coastal regions of the Caribbean, where African diseases reinforced the destructive power of those imported from Europe. Enslaved Africans, however, could and soon did provide a more disease-resistant labor force for plantation agriculture and other economic enterprises in the New World. Relatively precise calculation of the number of slaves carried from Africa is possible because the traffic came to be conducted by specialized slave ships, whose number and carrying capacity can be established with some accuracy. A recent estimate puts the number of Africans brought to the New World before 1820 at 7.8 million; and the same authority suggests that this figure is four to five times the contemporaneous total of European migration across the Atlantic.[21]

This perhaps surprising statistic ought to remind us of how important compulsory labor became and long remained in the New World. Compulsion bulks even larger in our perspective when we remember that most of the Europeans who crossed the Atlantic before steamships cheapened the cost of passage came as unfree indentured servants. Between 300,000 and 400,000 such persons left Britain for North America between 1650 and 1780, according to the best available estimates. This figure amounts to something between half and three-quarters of all the whites who came to North America from Europe before the American revolution.[22] Indentured servants could, of course, look forward to becoming free men if they survived the period of their indentured labor. But as long as their bondage lasted—often seven years—their legal position vis-à-vis their master was not much different from that of black slaves, though the absence of physical differentiation in outward appearance may have made it easier for them to run away before completing their contracts.

The free, egalitarian, and neo-barbarian style of frontier life, so dear to Turner and his followers, did of course exist in North America. It arose wherever export trade failed to thrive during the early stages of colonization. But in the more favored and accessible regions, where European skills proved capable of producing marketable wealth on a relatively large scale, frontier conditions ordinarily provoked not freedom but a social hierarchy steeper than anything familiar in Europe itself. The reason was that commercially precocious frontier societies usually found it necessary to assure the availability and subordination of a labor force by imposing stern legal restrictions on freedom to choose and change occupation. Hence, slave plantations and gangs of indentured servants in the Americas, as well as the serf-cultivated estates of eastern Europe, were quite as characteristic of the frontier as were the free and independent farmers and jacks-of-all-trades whom we habitually associate with frontier life.

One form of export trade that often played a prominent role on the frontier did impose a close symbiosis of equalitarian freedom with bureaucratic hierarchy. Capturing and collecting existing goods—whether furs, placer gold, raw rubber from the Amazon rain forest, or codfish from the Grand Banks—could only be done by a dispersed work force, operating beyond any manager's control. Trans-oceanic marketing of such goods, on the other hand, required comparatively large-scale organization.[23] Trading companies solved this problem by stationing agents at strategic locations, where they conducted a barter trade with the men who did the actual collecting. Commodities exchanged were sufficiently valuable to the parties concerned to bear the cost of transport; and even at remote locations, agents could still be controlled by their home offices since everyone knew that if they failed to send back adequate amounts of the sought-after commodity, the flow of trade goods needed for barter would promptly dry up.

Though a few big trading companies thus managed to span the forbidding distances between European metropolitan centers and the frontier, it remained the case that frontier conditions could not sustain the elaborately graded hierarchy that prevailed in the heartlands of European civilization. Near the center, long tradition and market constraints combined to fit men and women into an elaborately interlocking and largely hereditary pattern of occupations. Legal differentiation separated clergy, nobles, and commoners, and defined membership in a great variety of privileged corporations. In skilled trades, apprentices were bound to their masters for a period of years under conditions that somewhat resembled indentured labor in America. In all these senses, labor was subject to legal coercion in Europe too. But slavery was unimportant; serfdom had disappeared from the most active centers of European economic life long before Columbus sailed; and the price system, acting through fluctuating wages, was becoming increasingly effective in allocating and reallocating labor among competing occupations. Large-scale undertakings like mining and shipping could recruit the necessary manpower by offering appropriate rates of pay. Even soldiering had become a question of fulfilling a contract freely entered into, at least in principle; though once enlisted, a soldier, more even than an indentured servant or apprentice, faced severe penalties for seeking to withdraw from his place in the ranks.

Western Europe's reliance on the market as a means of allocating and reallocating labor among alternative employments was sustained by birth and survival rates that were high enough to supply hands for existing enterprises with a few left over for promising new ventures as well. Legal compulsion, backed by force, became quite unnecessary when enough labor presented itself spontaneously for carrying out all the tasks that the rulers and managers of society felt were really necessary and important. Under such circumstances, compulsion became a waste of time and effort, and a needless provocation as well.

The balance of supply and demand for labor was always precarious. The Black Death in the fourteenth century set back European population for more than a century and altered wage rates abruptly. Thereafter, recurrent epidemics, concentrated especially in towns, frequently cut back on local populations, sometimes very sharply.[24] But such perturbations were rapidly made good by accelerated influx from the healthier countryside, where all those youths who were unable to count on inheriting rights to enough cultivable land to live as their parents were doing constituted a pool of ready recruits for any venture that promised escape from what was, within the village confines, a radically unsatisfactory career prospect. Europe's remarkable record of expansion at home and abroad, dating back to about A.D. 900, rested on a demographic pattern that regularly provided a surplus of rural youths for export to towns and armies, with a few left over for migration to more distant frontier zones as well.

But Europe's demographic balance, elaborate social hierarchy, and the well-established interdependence of social classes could not be reproduced on the frontier. Local population was inadequate. Large-scale enterprise that required major input of labor could not be carried on without compulsion. This was as true of the overland as of the overseas frontier. The legal enserfment of Russian peasants in the seventeenth century differed only slightly from the slavery of American plantations; and debt peonage imposed on Amerindians in the New World, as well as English indentured labor, had the same practical effect, even if the obligated human beings retained rights under these legal systems that were denied to black slaves.

The whole point was to keep slaves, serfs, indentured servants, and peons at work on tasks a managerial, owning class wanted to see accomplished. In proportion to their success, a flood of new goods—sugar, cotton, silver, wheat, indigo, and many more—entered European and world markets. Income thus accruing to enterprising landowners, mine operators, and resident factors for wholesale merchants based in Europe allowed them to buy expensive imported European products so that they could live like gentlemen—more or less. In this fashion a slender simulacrum of European polite society quickly arose in American and European frontier lands. Subsequently, in proportion as local population grew so that labor became available for various crafts and retail commercial occupations, an approximation to European forms of society could gradually develop in the shadow of the planter-landowner-managerial class.

The prominence of slavery and serfdom in European frontier expansion did not foreclose the egalitarian alternative entirely, even in societies dominated by compulsory labor. Runaways and individuals who had worked out their indenture could and did take off into the backwoods to carve out a life free of any obligation to social superiors. Such pioneers often cut themselves off from any but sporadic contacts with civilization. But, like planters and landowners of the frontier, they continued to depend for some critically important items on sources of supply far in the rear. Guns and ammunition, as well as iron for tools, were things that even the most remote frontiersmen found it hard to do without. How they got possession of such goods is often unclear. Hand-to-hand swapping could reach far beyond organized markets; and incentive to swapping was real enough since the frontier could usually be made to yield something precious and portable—furs, placer gold, or the like—that commanded a high enough price on world markets to justify its carriage across many miles of plain and mountain.

Hence even the most remote and barbarous *coureurs de bois* of North America, the *bandierantes* of Brazil, the *gauchos* of the pampas, the *vortrekkers* of South Africa, and the Cossacks of Siberia retained a significant and vitally important link with the nearest outposts of civilization. Like the slave-owners and serf-owners of the frontier they, too, participated in the world market system that centered in western Europe. Their participation shrank in proportion as their mode of life descended toward local self-sufficiency. But complete autarky meant loss of the margin of superiority newcomers enjoyed vis-à-vis older native inhabitants. Those who cut loose entirely from Europe-centered and -managed trade nets simply merged into local indigenous populations, and thereupon ceased to act as agents of frontier expansion. Such persons were always few, since the status of a man without access to a gun (and other European-made goods) diminished drastically in remote communities.

The sharp polarization in frontier society between freedom and hierarchy should therefore be understood as arising from alternative responses to the overriding reality of the frontier, to wit, the drastic shortage of labor. For this reason, one social structure was capable of abrupt transmutation into its opposite. Runaway slaves or serfs who made good an escape

from their master's control at once became egalitarian frontiersmen. The maroons of Jamaica constituted the most famous such community, but were only one of many. On Europe's other flank, Cossack hordes in their early days recruited
runaway serfs as a matter of course; later, after the hordes
were themselves captured by the Russian state, such escape
became illegal, though successful flight into the depths of Siberia continued to occur as long as Russian serfdom endured.

The opposite transmutation from egalitarianism to legally
imposed hierarchy was even more common. In the east,
wholesale enserfment of once-free peasant populations was the
order of the day when frontier expansion into the steppelands
got seriously underway in the seventeenth and eighteenth centuries. In the New World, the rise of peonage in Mexico in
the sixteenth and seventeenth centuries was analogous. Efforts
to transplant reinvigorated forms of manorial jurisdiction to
Canada and New York met with scant success; and indentured
labor provided only a precarious basis for gentlemen farmers
in Virginia and Maryland in the seventeenth and eighteenth
centuries. But such efforts show that the urge to impose legal
bonds on free men operated in English, Dutch, and French
colonial society as well as on the Russian and Spanish frontiers.

We are accustomed to thinking of the equalitarian alternative as the norm of frontier life. Both Turner and Webb, for
example, skip over the role of slavery in the frontier history
of the United States. I suppose this remarkable omission arose
from the fact that they cherished an ideal of American liberty
and equality, and also felt nostalgia for the days of their youth
when residues of the Wisconsin and west Texas forms of frontier life still dominated local society. By noticing only one
aspect of frontier reality, Turner and Webb were able to combine these sentiments uninhibitedly. But this kind of wishful

thinking deserves to be subjected to skeptical examination. If one does so, it seems to me that a neutral observer would have to conclude that compulsion and legally reinforced forms of social hierarchy were more generally characteristic of frontier society than were equality and freedom.

Two reasons for this circumstance suggest themselves. First of all, free and equal nuclear families scattered thinly over the landscape are in a poor position to protect themselves. Consequently, wherever safeguard from enemy raiding parties was important, the radical equalitarianism of isolated pioneer homesteads proved inadequate. Even in the American west, the U.S. cavalry was called upon to shield settlers from raiding Indians. In the Old World, exposure to violence was far more serious, since, beginning in the 1480s, the Crimean Tartars organized systematic raids across the Ukrainian steppes to supply the insatiable Ottoman slave market. Scattered householders could not mount effective self-defense against such manhunts. Only specialized military organizations—whether the Cossack hordes or the Tsar's regular army—could confront raiding Tartars on more or less even terms. Consequently, for pioneering cultivators of the soil, the price of security from Tartar raids was subjection to experts in violence who could maintain an effective, professionalized frontier defense. Heartfelt efforts to reaffirm vanishing social equality and freedom within the framework of the Cossack horde were nullified by the fact that the Russian state made the horde itself into a privileged corporation after 1648. By exempting enrolled Cossacks from the obligations of serfdom, the Tsar acquired a new and formidable instrument for defending the frontier and imposing serfdom on the rest of the population of the Ukrainian borderlands. Thereafter, Tartar slave raids quickly ceased to be profitable, and the rich grasslands of the western steppe became safe for agricultural settlement on a massive scale.[25]

Because North America was less exposed to military threat than the Eurasian steppelands, American frontier experience gave more scope to the egalitarian, libertarian alternative than did the Russian. Important divergences in our societies still bear witness to this difference. But it was not the frontier per se that dictated this result. Instead it was our unusually low protection costs during the three centuries from 1608 to 1917. Australia, too, enjoyed negligible protection costs until even more recently than the United States, whereas Boer Vortrekkers encountered quite formidable rivals in the kaffir tribesmen with whom they disputed rights to land and water for nearly two centuries. Australia's populist egalitarianism was therefore free to flourish at the expense of imported hierarchies of class and culture, whereas Boer anarchic and egalitarian traditions were tempered by recurrent acceptance of military subordination to commanders whose authority was as great as it was temporary.

A second factor militating against equality and freedom on the frontier was economic. Dependence on supplies from the rear meant that pioneers were chronically at the mercy of merchants and suppliers who, by controlling transportation, controlled the terms of trade. When frontiersmen needed little, and rarely bought or sold anything, this did not infringe upon their liberty very much. But when buying and selling increased in importance so that everyday life began to depend on it, then the few who controlled access to distant markets were in a very favorable position to enhance their income at the expense of the ordinary farmer, miner or fur trapper.

In other words, land ownership and control over a labor force legally tied to the spot was not always necessary to allow a few to exploit the labor of others. This was the burden of populist protest against railroads and other outside capitalist interests that became such a prominent feature of United States politics in the second half of the nineteenth century. The Hudson's Bay Company, John Jacob Astor, and the Stroganov company that dominated the Siberian fur trade were no more popular with the backwoodsmen of an earlier age. London and Lisbon merchants who supplied Virginia planters and Brazilian slave owners had a similar relationship with their aristocratic trade partners, while the grain dealers and shipowners who carried grain from Danzig and Odessa to European markets were also in an advantageous position to dictate terms to Polish and Russian landowners.

In all such situations, traders with connections back to the distant markets and workshops of Europe represented the entering wedge for the social complexity and occupational differentiation that was and remained the special hallmark of civilization. Men who bought cheap and sold dear, and made chaffering over prices into a way of life, were disliked and even hated by frontier dwellers—rich and poor, owners and workers, free and bond. Recurrent pogroms against Jews in eastern Europe attest this fact all too poignantly. But frontiersmen could not get on without such people either. Goods otherwise inaccessible were too attractive and too important to do without, even if the purchaser felt cheated in every deal. The only alternative to importation was local manufacture: and in some Ukrainian towns as well as in American cities artisan trades had begun to take root before 1750. Social complexity grew accordingly. Little by little civilization was encroaching.

Nevertheless, prior to 1750 the replication of cosmopolitan complexity and of a graded hierarchy of social classes in peripheral regions of the European world system remained incomplete and sporadic. Until after that date the European empires arising from the first two modern centuries of expansion remained in place, and were, in fact, growing with each passing decade. That political fact registered the imperfect diffusion of civilized skills and techniques from center to periphery. After 1776, as the process of civilized expansion continued, political patterns changed, signaling a more complete transfer of the arts and skills of civilization onto new ground. In addition, a new demographic regime in Europe provided a basis for far more massive emigration than had previously occurred.

My next lecture will consider aspects of this second phase in the history of the Great Frontier.

LECTURE II: FROM 1750

THE FIRST of these lectures argued that frontier conditions distorted the social pyramid of European society either by flattening it drastically toward equality and anarchic freedom or, alternatively, by steepening the gradient so as to divide frontiersmen between owners and managers, on the one hand, and an enslaved, enserfed, or debt-coerced work force, on the other. The frontier in other words was neutral as between freedom and compulsion; but the actual balance tipped toward legally sharpened hierarchy because both the need for protection and the prospect of profit pulled in that direction. Before 1750 the freedom and equality we like to associate with frontier life were marginal. The norm was enslavement since only in that way could thinly populated frontier lands participate actively in the world market, and, if need be, also sustain a costly armed establishment.

The starkness of frontier alternatives began to soften after 1750. Two factors pushed in that direction. First of all, an ever-denser network of communication and transportation connecting the center to the periphery tended to flatten the cultural slopes within the European world system, reducing contrasts between each constituent part. Secondly, a new demographic regime accelerated population growth in most of the civilized world. This tended to diminish the labor shortages that had initially provoked both the anarchic and the authoritarian forms of frontier society.

Let me begin with some remarks about the second of these factors, for it was the onset of a new demographic regime about the middle of the eighteenth century which justifies dividing these lectures at the year 1750.

Demographic historians are far from agreed as to what may explain the onset of systematic population growth in the second half of the eighteenth century. But there is no longer any doubt that a change took place, not only in Europe but also in China and the Americas, and probably in India and Africa as well. Warmer and drier climate brought better harvests to northwestern Europe; but such an alteration in climate must have had diverse consequences for farming in other regions of the earth. In the Middle East, for instance, if it also became warmer and drier (which is not known to be the case), then the effect would be to damage crop yields and favor pastoralism. This may well have happened; evidence is simply not in hand. But since the Middle East does not seem to have shared in the rest of the world's eighteenth-century population increase, the hypothesis of an unfavorable climate change there is surely worth investigating along the lines that have been pioneered in Europe.[1]

Another factor operative throughout the Old World was the spread of American food crops as supplements to older kinds of nourishment. Maize, potatoes, sweet potatoes, peanuts, and tomatoes—to name but the most important—allowed peoples in China, Africa, Europe, and elsewhere to increase local production of food, sometimes very substantially. By interspersing old and new crops, as usually happened, risk of failure was diminished. Sometimes new crops did not displace old ones at all, since they could be grown on previously uncropped ground. In northern Europe, for example, it was possible to substitute potatoes for grain-fallow, thus abruptly increasing total food production. In China, too, sweet potatoes grew well on hilly ground that was unsuited to rice paddies. Even when this sort of pure gain was not feasible, American crops often improved the food supply because they yielded more calories per acre than anything known before. Maize was valued in Africa and southern Europe for this reason. Tomatoes, on the other hand, provided vitamins otherwise lacking, especially in Mediterranean and Indian diets. Almost everywhere, in short, American crops expanded available food supplies, sometimes very greatly. The catch was that the new crops required extra labor. They all had to be hoed and weeded during the growing season whereas wheat and other Old World grains (except rice) did not.

Without American food crops, the population growth that began in the Old World during the eighteenth century probably could not have continued for very long. But in and of itself, the availability of new, labor-intensive crops does not seem sufficient to explain systematic population growth, since, without an expanding supply of manpower, American crops could not have spread as fast and as far as they did.[2]

Historical demographers have therefore looked at changes in marriage age, fertility, and other indices of population dynamics. Meticulous and ingenious work with parish records in France and England has indeed shown some changes, but none seems adequate to account for systematic population increase all round the earth. What does appear from such studies, however, is a decrease in the severity of periodic die-off due to epidemic infection. In some instances improvements in medicine may have made a difference by reducing the ravages of plague and smallpox, but the most powerful explanation as to why epidemics became less destructive is to suppose that as communications nets became denser throughout the civilized world, an intensified circulation of lethal diseases left fewer adults at risk. Obviously, whenever lethal infections became endemic or returned at very frequent intervals, all but newborn infants and small children would already have been exposed. And for many infections, exposure provoked lifelong immunity. Lethality therefore concentrated among the very young. Replacement of such infant deaths was relatively easy and cost far less than was the case before the eighteenth century, when more sporadic communications left persons of childbearing years also exposed.[3]

Changes in human numbers resulting from the new demographic regime that set in after 1750 were drastic indeed. China's population doubled from about 150 million in 1700 to 313 million in 1794,[4] while Europe's population rose from about 118 million in 1700 to about 187 million in 1801. Within Europe, the most rapid growth came on the two flanks. In Great Britain, population swelled from about 5.8 million in 1700 to 9.15 million in 1801, while Russia's population increased from about 12.5 million in 1724 to some 21 million in 1796.[5]

Still more spectacular was the rate of demographic expansion that took place in the Americas and along Russia's steppe frontier. In some Ukrainian districts, for example, population tripled in the eighteenth century through a combination of immigration and natural increase. In the Americas modest immigration from Europe continued throughout the eighteenth century, but spectacular rates of natural increase accounted for most of the expansion of the white population. The population of the English mainland colonies in North America, for example, grew from about 350,000 in 1700 to no less than 5 million in 1800![6] More interesting, perhaps, is the fact that the die-off of Indian peoples, which had been such an important factor in initial encounters between Old and New World populations, bottomed out about a century and a half after contacts were initiated. As a result, in Mexico and Peru Indian and mestizo populations began to grow rapidly by the last decades of the eighteenth century, and at a pace that soon equalled or exceeded the rate of white population growth.

Enslaved African populations were not self-sustaining in

tropical regions; in the mainland colonies of North America, on the other hand, population growth among slaves also set in during the eighteenth century at a rate not much inferior to that of the white population.[7] Die-off continued to destroy isolated Indian tribes whenever white men inaugurated contact with them—a process continuing into the twentieth century. But the initial catastrophe in the heavily populated regions of the New World had passed by 1700 or before. With this, new patterns of encounter began among the diverse ethnic groups of the New World—a process we today are still trying to get used to in the United States.

The global or nearly global disturbance to older population equilibria which manifested itself in the eighteenth century was a fundamental destabilizer of human affairs thereafter. Something over 90 percent of the earth's population lived by working the soil when the process began. Population growth therefore initially meant finding ways to accommodate young persons as they attained marriageable age within the framework of existing rural society. When adequate land lay close at hand and property rights did not interfere, a growing population simply meant expansion of tillage; and until that sort of internal colonization began to bring marginal lands under cultivation, local village living standards and styles of life did not need to alter very much.

When the eighteenth-century population growth set in, cultivable land *did* lie within easy reach of established village communities in most parts of the earth. This was generally the case in Latin America, for example, where earlier Amerindian die-off had emptied vast stretches of good land. Cultivable land was probably available in vast areas of India and Africa as well. The same was certainly true in eastern Europe, where peasant occupancy of the landscape remained comparatively thin. In these regions, therefore, the onset of the new demographic regime after 1750 made little difference at first. As each new generation came of age, new fields could be found for them to cultivate. Their presence enhanced the total wealth of society and sustained a continued growth of political and commercial networks. Often, from the peasants' point of view, there was a price to pay in the form of harsher subjection to landowners who could choose among competing bidders for access to land they controlled. But frictions over how to divide a growing total production were not very acute as long as new fields kept up with new mouths to feed.

In other regions of the earth, however, more drastic changes were triggered by the new population pattern. Wherever cultivators had already occupied almost all of the fertile soil, a hard choice confronted young people as they came of age. Either they could stay in place, with the prospect of inheriting only a share of their parents' holdings, or they could leave the familiar environment in which they had grown up, and seek a better future somewhere else.

When new crops and techniques were available, subdividing peasant holdings could proceed without putting such a strain on older living standards and expectations as to be unacceptable. This seems to have happened in much of China, for example, as well as in some regions of western Europe. In Java this pattern went to unparalleled extremes, thanks to the remarkable responsiveness of paddy fields to intensified labor inputs, and to a social system that "developed into a dense web of finely spun work rights and work responsibilities spread, like the reticulate veins of the hand, throughout the whole body of the village lands."[8] Irish peasants, by exploiting the fact that a single acre of potatoes could feed an entire family, did much the same before the catastrophic potato famine hit in 1845-1847, while at the other end of Europe, Rumanian peasants came to depend on the other great American staple, maize, so completely as to become liable to pellagra. No doubt other rural communities, e.g., in India and Japan, also responded to growing population by what Clifford Geertz aptly christened "agricultural involution."

A second and in many ways more successful, because more elastic, response to population pressure on the land was to go in for handicraft manufacture. This allowed extra hands to survive in the village by supplementing agricultural with industrial sources of income. Assuredly, wherever villages were already in contact with a commercial network, rising rural populations put serious new pressures on guild and other urban manufacturing monopolies. In many parts of Europe, rural industry was already centuries old. It dated back, largely, to an earlier age of population crunch when, before the Black Death, the peasants of England, the Low Countries, and adjacent parts of Europe broke through urban monopolies by going in for the manufacture of cheap textiles. This pattern intensified in the eighteenth century and spread to new ground, e.g., to Ulster and Silesia, where linen-weaving began to sustain dense, poverty-stricken multitudes.

But for us, trying to understand what transpired along the frontiers of an expanding European world, what mattered most was the alternative to domestic manufacture and/or agricultural involution, i.e., migration.

The easiest kind of migration was short-range: from village to town. Such a flow was as old as civilization itself, because towns and cities were places of demographic decay due to intensified infection. Until modern sewage systems and other public health measures took effect in the second half of the nineteenth century, urban populations could not sustain themselves biologically without recruitment from the healthier countryside. But the systematically accelerated influx beginning to descend upon the towns of western Europe in the last decades of the eighteenth century, created immediate problems. No adequate livelihood automatically offered itself for the flood of newcomers.

One response was riot and protest. In France this allowed the dynamic of the French Revolution to run its remarkable course. Domestic riot and constitutional upheaval gave way after 1792 to civil and foreign war; and the emergency of 1793 occasioned the famous *levée en masse* whereby otherwise underemployed young men were recruited into the army. This proved an efficacious way of relieving population pressure in France. Army deaths very nearly equalled natural increase in the years of Napoleon's campaigns. Demobilization in 1815 had another unexpected by-product, for methods of birth control (perhaps propagated by army experiences of sex) became sufficiently widespread in postwar France to affect the further growth of population in that country. This distinguished France from adjacent parts of Europe, where far higher rates of natural increase continued to prevail until near the end of the century.

More important for the world as a whole was the eighteenth-century response of Great Britain to the accelerated urban influx of employable young people. A generation of expert study of the causes of the commercial and industrial changes that began to assume revolutionary proportions in Great Britain after about 1780 now seems to have reached consensus about the centrality of population growth in provoking the Industrial Revolution.[9] The role of population pressure in precipitating the political and military upheavals of the French Revolution and Napoleonic Wars is far less firmly grounded in existing historiography, but will, I think, soon become a cliché of European history if ideological pieties do not interfere.[10]

As we all know, once the shocks of the Napoleonic Wars

had passed, the industrial and commercial transformation of European society gained momentum and began to spread beyond British borders. New technology soon improved transportation fundamentally: first steamships, then railroads. Older limits on movement of men and commodities were left far behind as fossil fuels enlarged the energies that human beings could call upon at will. The result was to facilitate movement to and fro within an expanding Europe-centered world system, and to project an ever-larger number of disease-experienced persons into remote corners of the earth, where their encounters with previously isolated communities promoted die-offs and created vast new frontiers for Europeans to develop. South Africa, Australia, and Oceania were thereby added to North and South America as theaters for European settlement; and rapidly growing populations in the densely occupied parts of western (and ere long of central and eastern) Europe provided a stock of would-be migrants, whenever obstacles of cost and ignorance of the unknown could be overcome.

How, then, were these new dynamics of human ecology registered along the frontiers? What happened to the older antithetical complementarity between egalitarian anarchy and legally enforced subordination? Needless to say, each place and time was different. Variability, reaching down to the roles of individuals in particular actions and situations, was infinite. This dimension of the historical past ought not to be swept under the rug by attempts such as mine to look at the broad picture, searching for patterns of such generality as to lose touch with individual and local uniqueness. General and particular genuinely coexist, and when accurately discerned are equally true. Anyone who has looked at a landscape from the top of a tall building or from an airplane as well as from the ground will surely believe this to be so. With this nod to the microhistorical approach to reality, let me climb back into orbit and try to answer the question: What difference did the post-1750 demographic regime make along Europe's far-flung frontiers?

Overall and in the long run, the effect of demographic growth and cheapened transport after 1750 was to reduce differences between center and periphery. But this took time, and whenever a newly emptied frontier opened, the initial stark contrast between freedom and hierarchy reappeared, sometimes briefly, sometimes enduring down to the present. In Australia, for example, the contrast between the lawless bushrangers of the Outback and the prison regimen imposed on the convict labor supplied to New South Wales between 1788 and 1840 was as stark as the contrast between New World slavery and freedom—and a good deal more violent.[11]

In South Africa too, the Boers, who successfully pioneered a mainly pastoral style of life on the veld during the course of the eighteenth century, enslaved the native Hottentots, whose vulnerability to imported diseases resembled that of other isolated populations. When, however, Boer pioneers collided with Bantu-speaking "kaffirs" the terms of epidemiological encounter altered, inasmuch as the Bantu were about as disease-experienced as the Dutch, and enjoyed much the same technological and epidemiological superiority over Hottentots as did the Boers.

The superiority of gun to spear therefore became decisive along the frontier where these two expanding peoples met, clashing for the first time in 1702. Repeated bloody encounters set in during the 1770s, and lasted for a full century. (The Zulu war of 1879 was the last major struggle.) At stake was the right to land and access to water holes. Wherever whites prevailed they took possession of the good land. African tribal society retreated into refuge areas, where agriculture was precarious owing to recurrent droughts. But the land the Boers appropriated was not completely cleared of kaffirs. Individuals and families left behind when the tribes went down in defeat were put to work by the new landowners, who thereby escaped the indignity of manual labor. Forms of engagement differed from the convict labor of Australia, but the reality of compulsion backed by legal forms and military force was not fundamentally different.

Yet among themselves the Boers were stubbornly egalitarian and anarchic. As free men they clashed repeatedly with British officials' efforts after 1805 to introduce regular administration, protect native rights, and impose taxes. Hence frontier freedom and hierarchy coexisted in South Africa in a peculiarly intense fashion that persists down to our own time.[12]

Between 1750 and 1850, therefore, Australia and South Africa recapitulated, with variations of their own, the familiar frontier pattern of sharp social polarization. Nor did similar polarities disappear from the Americas. They were in fact reborn with every new advance of the frontier from the first zones of encounter. Thus, for example, Brazilian sugar plantations, based on slavery and usually situated fairly near the coast, were supplemented in the eighteenth century by important inland mines where enslaved Negroes and Indians provided much of the labor for digging gold and diamonds from the ground. But, like the Boers of South Africa, the most inveterate Brazilian pioneers, the Paulistas, were themselves belligerently egalitarian and all but ungovernable, save when they voluntarily formed themselves into quasi-military bands for ventures deep into the interior. Their exploration and slave raiding expanded Brazil's territory deep into the hinterland, and provoked a long series of clashes with Spaniards and other European rivals. Runaway slaves were also able to form a polity of their own in the Brazilian backwoods, but between 1772 and 1794 Paulista *bandierantes* destroyed this rival to their dominion by persistent armed attacks.[13]

In North America, slave plantations in Alabama, Mississippi, and east Texas shared in the frontier movement across the continent until 1865. And, at the libertarian extreme, free and equal agricultural pioneers living in isolated cabins were matched by the competitive anarchy of pioneer gold miners in California and Colorado, and the counter-culture of such specialized frontier populations as the buffalo-hunting *metis* of Manitoba, whose armed collision with Canadian authorities in 1885 has become part of French Canadian hagiography.[14]

An important variant of frontier patterns of life, deliberately omitted from my first lecture, was illustrated anew by the Mormon trek to Utah in 1846-1847. Brigham Young and the eleven other Apostles of the new faith replicated in essentials what the Pilgrim Fathers of Massachusetts had achieved some two centuries before. For, like the Puritan leaders of the seventeenth century, Mormon church authorities managed to impose a stern discipline upon their followers. This, in turn, allowed them to transplant a tight-knit community, numbering thousands, from Illinois to Utah. Far-ranging, quasi-military subordination of ordinary believers to church authorities made the feat possible. Yet obedience in all the strenuous shared labors of building Zion in the wilderness was freely rendered in nearly every case.

The Mormons' remarkable social discipline was sustained by the fact that irrigation agriculture, upon which the main body came to depend, required common effort and centralized control. Isolated households could not hope to achieve comparable success in harnessing the streams descending from the mountains into the desert basin of Utah. Thus the technical conditions of life in the new community sustained and reinforced the religious bonds that made large-scale exploitation of water resources possible in the first place.[15]

In this respect, the Mormons were more fortunate than their Puritan forerunners, for the subsistence farming of New England, conducted by independent nuclear families, benefited only marginally from any kind of collective effort and therefore remained technically quite independent of public authority. For that reason, perhaps, the theocracy of Massachusetts did not endure for as long as a century, whereas the Latter-Day Saints of Jesus Christ, to give the Mormons their proper name, continue to flourish and still manage to maintain remarkable cohesiveness, despite the clashes with federal authorities in the last decades of the nineteenth century that resulted in dismantlement of the collective polity that Brigham Young had erected.

Sectarian communities organized and disciplined by religious faith and subordinated to ecclesiastical leaders also flourished along the Russian frontier. Some were foreign, like the German Mennonites who succeeded in setting up prosperous agricultural communities along the banks of the Don and Volga in the eighteenth century. More important for Russia as a whole were dissidents within the Orthodox faith itself, the so-called Old Believers. Persecution by Russian churchmen drove many of the Old Believers toward remote forests and marginal steppelands where the writ of the Russian government ceased to run. In the north, refugees from persecution succeeded in setting up some remarkable communities that supplemented what they could raise and gather from infertile soils with manufacture of ironware and other handicrafts. They also devised a surprisingly elaborate, far-ranging trade system so as to be able to bring back enough grain to make good the shortfall of their own harvests. As a result, Old Believers became pioneers of Russian industry and commerce in quite disproportionate degree.

Official persecution relaxed in the eighteenth century only to intensify anew in the twentieth. As a result, some of the Russian Mennonites and Old Believers found it prudent to colonize selected spots along the American frontier, scattering themselves all the way from Argentina and Paraguay in the south to the United States and Canada in the north. In the New World these sects soon replicated, though in somewhat softened form, the collisions with constituted authority that had so often distinguished them in Russia.[16]

Frontier sectarianism could also assume more grisly form. In South Africa, for example, Bantu tribesmen slaughtered their cattle and consumed their seed corn in 1857 on the strength of a religious revelation that promised spiritual replenishment of the land and its purgation of whites. Mass starvation ensued.[17] In Brazil, a generation later, a millenarian cult formed around a wild holy man who was called "Good Jesus Comforter" by his followers. They took to arms and soon provoked war to the death with state authorities. After two years of fighting the struggle ended in 1897 with the total massacre of the defiant believers.[18] More recently, in 1978, the mass suicide of Jim Jones's followers, who had gone pioneering in the hostile environment of the Guyana rain forest, shocked American public opinion with a macabre exhibition of how far a search for freedom through voluntary submission to religious authority can go. Such (only seemingly) paradoxical behavior has always been peculiarly at home along the frontier. There men are few so that scoffing unbelievers cannot do much to threaten the community of the faithful, whereas cooperative effort, sustained by common belief, permits practical achievements far beyond anything isolated pioneer families can accomplish by themselves.

In these and other instances, frontier society in Eurasia and the Americas continued to exhibit the tension between op-posites that is characteristic of regions where land abounds while people and skills are in short supply. Anarchic freedom and artificially reinforced social hierarchy continued to mix like fire and water throughout the moving frontier zones of the earth after, as well as before, 1750.

The new element in east European and in American society that assumed growing importance after the middle of the eighteenth century was characteristic, instead, of our effete east. For along the Atlantic coast of this country, at the centers of political management in Latin America and in cities of the Ukraine, Rumania, and Hungary, complexly stratified social structures approximating more and more closely to west European patterns began to flourish. Philadelphia, New York and Boston, Budapest, Bucharest and Kiev, Mexico City, Lima and Buenos Aires—to name but a few of the key centers— began to play the role of metropolis to their respective hinterlands more and more adequately as population grew and skills increased. Occupational differentiation like that of European cities proliferated. Varying wage rates became capable of apportioning labor among competing occupations more and more effectively. Severe legal penalties for changing jobs no longer were necessary to get nasty tasks done. Serfdom and slavery therefore became dispensable, though a century and more passed before the law fully ratified this changing social reality.

The American War of Independence and the establishment of a new sovereign government on American soil (1776-1789) hastened the process of transferring the full panoply of European civilization to the New World. Latin America lagged only slightly behind, for Spain's American empire was reduced to a few tattered fragments between 1808 and 1821, and Brazil also became independent in 1822, though it remained under the rule of a branch of the Portuguese royal house until 1889.

Self-government and all the trappings of sovereignty generated new occupations and a new spirit as well. But exact replication of Europe was never in question. If nothing else, race mixture in the Americas guaranteed enduring differences. Relations between Amerindian or largely Amerindian segments of the population and descendants of European and African immigrants worked themselves out in varying ways in different parts of the New World. In Haiti, blacks displaced all others; in New England whites did the same. But in most regions black, white, and red shared the ground in varying proportions with an ever-rising number of persons of mixed blood.

As long as fresh land could readily be found for youths reaching marriageable age, population growth presented no really critical problems. In the United States and Canada, the politically volatile issues everywhere turned on relations between urban centers, where the new managerial elites concentrated, and rural folk. In remoter parts of Latin America, Amerindian villagers continued to pursue a subsistence pattern of life almost unaffected by outsiders; but in central Mexico and other regions closer to urban markets and political seats of power, disruptive intervention of the market and of individuals with access to legal devices for extending their control over land divided society into hostile and more or less uncomprehending rival camps.

But even in such cases, the long-term effect of improved transportation and communications—the railroad, telegraph, newspaper, and all their twentieth-century equivalents—was to narrow the gap between town and country by enlarging the scale of market transactions in rural life. Galloping commercialization, in turn, generated political frictions, because the rural partners felt aggrieved by unfavorable terms of trade. The upshot, overall, was to bring erstwhile frontier societies closer to the European metropolitan pattern and at a relatively rapid rate.

Perhaps the most obvious register of the diminishing difference between the social structures of the European center and the frontier societies of the earth was the legal abolition of serfdom and slavery that occurred during the nineteenth century. This was a step-by-step process of course, since different sovereignties held jurisdiction. The earliest landmark was the prohibition of slavery within Great Britain in 1772, achieved by judicial interpretation rather than through formal legislation. Beginning with Vermont in 1777, some states within the new American union prohibited slavery by formal legislation, and so did the French revolutionary Convention in 1794. The Convention's act affected French possessions overseas, most notably Haiti, where a bloody insurrection was required to prevent Napoleon from reinstating slavery. Next, slavery was abolished throughout the British empire in 1833 by Act of Parliament. Thereafter the Royal Navy attempted to police the seas in order to intercept slave ships. Within two decades the Atlantic trade in slaves had been effectively halted; but not until the 1890s did slaving on Africa's east coast come completely to an end.

Only in the United States did the abolition of slavery involve large-scale resort to armed force. The Civil War (1861-1865) may not have turned solely on slavery, but surely that was the central issue throughout.[19] Thereafter, Brazil remained the principal slaveholding country in the Americas. Abolition came there peaceably in 1888. Ten years later, after the British had intervened in Zanzibar to stop that island from exporting slaves to Arab lands, African slavery became only a memory.

On Europe's eastern flank parallel legal changes took place during the same decades. The serfdom that had been instituted in the fifteenth, sixteenth, and seventeenth centuries to attach labor to the soil, so that landowners could increase their export of grain to western markets, was dismantled in the course of the nineteenth century. The process began when Prussia's defeat at Jena (1806) provoked reformers to abolish serfdom as part of that country's program of regeneration. A second wave of revolutionary reform led to the elimination of obligatory labor throughout the Hapsburg empire in 1848. Russia followed suit in 1861, and the last surviving bastion of serfdom disappeared from European soil in 1864 when Rumania did likewise.[20]

The end of these legal systems sanctioning compulsory labor outside and beyond market-regulated contracts did much to narrow the gap between frontier societies and the social structures at the centers of European civilization. But peonage remained important in Mexico and other parts of Latin America until the twentieth century, and contract labor, entered into by human beings who lacked familiarity with European law and custom, often resembled slavery very closely. It is therefore a mistake to suppose that legally sanctioned compulsory labor disappeared with the abolition of serfdom and slavery.

Australian history illustrates this very clearly. The last convicts were sent from Britain to Australia in 1867, cutting off the supply of prisoners' labor that had hitherto played a considerable role in getting things done "down under." Labor-short sugar plantations in Queensland thereupon met their problem by importing indentured laborers from the Solomon Islands under conditions approximating slavery. But the grant of self-government to the Australian colonies in 1850 had the effect of obstructing wholesale resort to indentured labor and assured that a "white Australia" policy would prevail. Chinese coolie immigration, begun at the time of the Australian gold rush in 1851, was stopped by legislative action in 1855, for example; and permanent residence was rigorously denied to the "kanakas" who continued to work on sugar plantations in the north.

The activities of the Belgian King Leopold's agents in the Congo, which became an international scandal in the first decade of this century, offer a better-known example of how compulsory labor could be prolonged beyond the time when legal prohibition of slavery had been written into European law and opinion. In South Africa, too, what amounted to compulsory labor survived by assuming new legal forms after the 1860s, when the discovery of gold and diamonds put sudden new pressures on older social and political patterns. Technical requirements for deep-rock mining dictated large-scale corporate organization; but the resulting super-modern style of business management proved compatible with a radically discriminatory labor system that paid high wages to unionized white miners and kept black African wages low. This was possible because the breakdown of tribal discipline combined with population pressure in the native reserves to create an African labor force that in practice had to accept almost any terms of employment the mining companies offered. South Africa therefore maintained into the last decades of the twentieth century an exploitative system of labor whose equivalent had disappeared almost everywhere else.[21]

But, for all their notoriety, exploitative labor contracts in South Africa and the Congo were statistically less important than the global deployment of Indian indentured labor, both within India and in various remote tropical regions of the globe. There is, indeed, some irony in the fact that the abolition of slavery throughout the British empire in 1833 set the scene for a vast increase in the employment of "coolie" labor to perform all the tasks that could not be accomplished by reliance on some more locally available work force. Indentured Indians in effect replaced enslaved Africans wherever British (and sometimes French) enterprise needed extra hands in tropical lands.

Within India itself, the coolie labor system sustained a continued frontier expansion. For, beginning in the 1840s and continuing until the 1920s, when the pressure of Indian public opinion led to the abolition of the system, tea plantations employed coolies to penetrate the virgin jungles of Assam in the best frontier tradition. Planters recruited their labor from crowded Indian villages by offering five-year indentures. Consequently, in the decade 1911-1921, when tea production in Assam reached its height, no fewer than 769,000 Indians were imported to that province under conditions that amounted to slavery. Actual working conditions on the tea plantations may in fact have been harsher than most forms of slavery, for the employers had no long-term stake in keeping their work force healthy; and the warm, wet climate allowed a formidable array of tropical diseases to afflict the imported workers.[22]

Elsewhere in the British empire, in Mauritius, Trinidad, Ceylon, Natal, etc., indentured laborers from India also played an important role in the nineteenth and early twentieth centuries. Altogether, 27.7 million Indians left the country between 1835 and 1920, nearly all of them as members of coolie gangs. About 24 million returned at the expiration of their contracts. Most of the remainder died, but a few lived on and their descendants constitute a distinct element in the local populations to the present.[23] Comparable statistics from China do not exist, but Chinese coolies were far fewer. Nonetheless, Chinese indentured laborers played a prominent part in the Australian gold rush (1851-1856), and gangs of Chinese coolies dug guano in Peru (1840s-1870s) and built the first railroads in California (1860s) and western Canada (1880s). Australia's "whites only" policy meant that all the Chinese had to go home; but in North America some remained behind when their work contracts expired, thus starting up the well-known Chinese communities of San Francisco and Vancouver.

The survival of thinly disguised forms of compulsion for mustering labor on the fringes of European expansion should not surprise us. There was no other way that the sugar industry could continue to thrive, or that railroad building and other large-scale construction projects could be carried through in places where local populations were scant or felt no incentive to alter their accustomed ways of life to work for white intruders. Moreover, the process fed on itself. Dock and railroad construction in remote places opened new possibilities for profitable mining and plantation enterprises, provided that a suitable work force could be brought to the scene. Coolies served the purpose as well or better than slaves could have done, since the temporary character of the engagement and the vestigial voluntarism of signing on made hard conditions seem both morally defensible to employers and bearable to the workers.

Yet, even though coolie labor became a really big business and carried nearly three times as many persons across the world's oceans as ever left Africa in Atlantic slave ships, legally sanctioned compulsion as a way of getting things done was nonetheless a diminishing, retreating mode of labor organization in the nineteenth and twentieth centuries. This was so because enslaved and indentured labor was dwarfed by a mass migration from Europe that set in after 1840.

Earlier migrations of free men from Europe went largely unrecorded, but by the time this mass movement got underway the diligence of modern governments resulted in the collection of relatively exact figures. We therefore know that about 46.2 million Europeans took up residence overseas between 1846 and 1920. More than 10 million others pioneered eastward in Siberia and the Caucasus lands during the latter part of that same period—mainly between 1880 and 1914.[24] Transoceanic movement of coolie labor amounted to about half as much during the same period of time. Free labor thus overbalanced compulsory labor decisively in the continuing economic development of European frontier and ex-frontier lands after the middle of the nineteenth century; whereas, as we saw in the first lecture, before 1800 the balance tilted quite the other way, since African slaves far outnumbered Europeans among immigrants to the Americas; and a large proportion of the Europeans who crossed the ocean did so as unfree indentured servants.

The brief extraordinary surge (1840-1920) of freely undertaken long-distance migration, financed individually or within small kinship groups, was a remarkable phenomenon in world history, and quite without parallel. It bulks so large in the national consciousness of the United States that many people assume it to be the normal form of human migration. But this is profoundly erroneous. Migrations that mattered, i.e., those that were successful in transplanting a population to new ground, have nearly always been conducted by organized groups, armed and prepared to repel the natives whose land they proposed to take over. The Biblical account of winning the Promised Land is therefore a far better model for the history of human migration than the pattern that prevailed in the nineteenth and twentieth centuries.

Individual and familial management of what became a mass movement was, indeed, so exceptional as to require special explanation. We can discern four unusual circumstances that came together to permit so vast an outpouring. First, steamships (from the 1840s) and then railroads (from the 1850s) made long-distance travel cheaper, faster, and far more capacious than before. Simultaneously, improved communications made reasonably accurate information available in European towns and villages about attractive conditions of life overseas or along the Siberian railroad. Thirdly, receiving lands welcomed newcomers because local managerial elites realized that immigrant labor would accelerate economic growth of a kind that they and nearly everyone else on the scene could expect to benefit from. Finally, a widespread population crunch in European villages supplied millions of young persons who were willing to seek their fortunes in distant lands because nothing satisfactory seemed possible at home.

As I remarked before, during the eighteenth century, when the modern population surge first began to affect Europe, in most places extra young people could make a satisfactory living simply by clearing new fields from waste and pasture lands lying close by. After the middle of the nineteenth century, however, in more and more parts of Europe, this simple response to rising numbers became impractical because all readily cultivable land had been taken up. Emigration therefore offered an obvious and increasingly accessible escape from an otherwise desperate *cul-de-sac*.

Of course, long-distance migration remained expensive even when steamships and railroads had done all they could to reduce transport costs. Millions of European peasants overcame this obstacle by using kinship ties to create and sustain a flow of migration from their overcrowded villages to hospitable communities overseas. Initial lodgment was always difficult and problematic. Exceptional individual enterprise or some unusual concatenation of circumstance was often necessary to plant the first emigrant from a given village in a distant and propitious spot where he could prosper. But when that occurred, the prospering newcomer, whether in the United States, Canada, Argentina, Australia, or somewhere else, commonly sent money back home in order to bring close relatives to wherever he had set himself up. Each newly arrived person could then do likewise, creating a chain of migration that might endure for several generations. Such arrangements allowed a large number of European villages to establish overseas extensions of the home community that sometimes far outnumbered those remaining behind. After the 1880s, when good agricultural land had nearly all been occupied overseas, these immigrant communities congregated in cities for the most part. Yet even in such radically alien environments village, regional, and especially religious ties from the old country allowed the migrants to retain a sense of collective identity and social control, at least for the first generation.

Not all of the Europeans who crossed the oceans after 1840 did so as fully free persons. Some depended on employers or labor contractors to pay their fares, and arrived at their destinations with the legal obligation to pay back the sums advanced, usually by agreeing to work for the person who had financed the passage. Like the contractors who provided Indian coolie labor in the tropics, bosses who recruited European manpower for remote mining and construction enterprises in temperate zones were not overscrupulous in their treatment of the people they carried across the sea. One of my own ancestors, for example, was shipped round the Horn to Vancouver Island sometime in the 1860s to mine coal for the Royal Navy; and if oral tradition is to be trusted, the conditions of life he left behind in Scotland and those he met with in British Columbia were about equally grim.

All the same, the enhanced possibility for voluntary emigration that set in after 1840 clearly tipped the balance between freedom and compulsion as the predominant mode of organizing work throughout the far-flung frontier lands open to European settlement. The influx of Irish and German, and then of Italian and Slavic immigrants, supplementing a continued flow from Great Britain itself, confirmed and expanded the predominance within the United States of market relationships and individual freedom as the way of staffing any and every sort of enterprise, large or small, public or private. Resulting rapid economic growth more than justified the abolition of slavery in 1863.[25] Chile, Brazil, and Argentina, together with Australia, New Zealand, Canada, and South Africa, became other important receivers of the swarming Europeans. In these countries, too (with the partial exception of South Africa and after the final abolition of slavery in Brazil in 1888) free choice of employment prevailed within limits set by a market operating with remarkably little legal restriction.

There was a catch to the new weight that individual choice and private decision-making came to have in peopling the frontiers of the earth. Some European villages (in south Italy, for example) were devitalized and well-nigh destroyed by losing too many of their inhabitants to America before 1914. Moreover, in the new lands to which the emigrants went, inequities and exploitation of the weak by the strong played variously ugly roles. Settlers eager to set up as farmers or in some other occupation within easy reach of the new railroads did not escape intimate involvement in the worldwide commercial network that sustained European civilization, nor did they wish to do so. But inasmuch as their new life depended on large-scale buying and selling, these latter-day pioneers found themselves very much at the mercy of middlemen who controlled the movement of goods to and from the regions where they had located.

Clashes of interest were built into this situation. Consequently, populist protest in the United States and comparable movements based in the hinterlands of other frontier countries played a very prominent part in late nineteenth- and early twentieth-century politics. Not until World War I did the gap between commercial and rural occupations and ways of life begin to narrow in the United States, as farmers became more urbanized in outlook and began to treat farming as a business. In Canada, Australia, New Zealand, and Argentina the commercialization of agriculture moved more or less *pari passu* with the transformation of rural life in the United States. The frontier heritage of differentiation and distrust between center and periphery faded proportionately.

After World War II even the ambivalences between freedom and compulsion characteristic of company towns at remote mining sites diminished markedly. Military experience in managing troops stationed at isolated outposts provided a model and standard for postwar civilian enterprise. As a result, since the 1950s miners and construction workers, even when employed at the ends of the earth, in remote Arctic locations or on deserts of the Persian Gulf, could fly in and out at frequent intervals. Such workers therefore kept effectively in touch with a larger world where free markets were more of a reality than could ever be the case in places where there was only one employer and only one supplier of outside goods.[26]

Recent developments within the vast reaches of the Russian empire also narrowed the gap between rural and urban, agricultural and industrial, ways of life. But in an interesting sense, in Russia it was the rural rather than the urban element that predominated in the amalgam.

The role of the market and of individual choice always remained slender in the Russian lands. Even after the abolition of serfdom in 1861, free contracts and a privately operated market in goods and services had only a comparatively modest development in Russia. Governmental decisions and bureaucratic initiatives mattered far more than in western countries, both before and after 1917. The Russian Revolution had the effect of enhancing the role of compulsion once more. War, communism (1917-1921), and the Five Year plans that started in 1928 mustered the labor force required for military and industrial undertakings by the old-fashioned method of issuing commands, backed by the threat and sometimes by the exercise of force. The change was most dramatically registered on the far margins of Russian society, where pioneering in the harsh climate of Siberia came to depend almost wholly on convict labor, directed by the secret police.

But lest we congratulate ourselves too warmly on the newly conspicuous gap between Soviet compulsion and our own greater reliance or private response to market incentives, let me conclude by pointing out that since the 1880s American society, too, has come increasingly under the influence of bureaucratic management. At first it was the bureaucracies of private corporations that mattered most.[27] But since the 1930s, governmental bureaucrats, allied with labor and business bureaucrats, have taken over primacy in regulating the lives of nearly all United States citizens.

No doubt, indirect controls of the sort favored in the United States are less galling than overt compulsion, but they are not altogether different either. A complex, differentiated, flow-through economy, staffed by diverse ethnic and religious groups who are united more by propinquity than by any obvious cultural uniformity, probably requires management by some kind of power elite. Certainly, traditional empires in the deeper past were managed in that way. The world market of the eighteenth and nineteenth centuries was also managed in important degree by a small number of bankers, merchants, politicians, and officials, nearly all of whom were based in western Europe. Indeed, the price of complete personal freedom is to consume only what one can produce for oneself in a place where risk of armed attack by outsiders has somehow been effectually exorcised. Such places are far and few in our world; and the actual cost in material terms of withdrawal from dependence on market relations for the supply of human wants is far more than even the most incandescent rebels of the 1960s were willing to pay.

·   ·   ·

THE history of the Great Frontier, as I see it, shows that the rewards of interdependence and exchange are too great to be foregone. But interdependence implies social hierarchy and management based on some mix of compulsion and incentive. Frontiersmen of the past acknowledged these realities, however begrudgingly, by their acts. None, or almost none, severed connection entirely with the civilized body whence they derived their skills and knowledge. They depended on supply from the rear for weapons and tools; and when improved communications in the nineteenth century established closer connections with civilized centers, few resisted the advantages which a broadened participation in market transactions offered, even when the terms of trade seemed systematically unfair.

The history of the United States, like the history of other lands brought within the circle of western European civilization in the past four hundred years, clearly registers these preferences. On an even grander scale, the history of humanity across the past five thousand years attests to the advantages of membership in civilized society, despite inherent inequalities and all the constraints on freedom that such membership entails.

Measured against such a time scale, the frontier phenomenon with which we have here been concerned appears as a remarkable but transitory wound, arising as a result of a demographic and cultural catastrophe to the normal equilibrium of the human ecosystem. Signs that the regimen of the past five hundred years is at an end are not wanting. For the process through which Europeans created the Great Frontier and occupied so many lands wound down very fast after 1914. World War I interrupted the flood of European emigration, and during the 1920s quota systems imposed by receiving countries prevented resumption of migration on the prewar scale.

Instead, changes in European family patterns and sex habits lowered the birth rate. As a result, except for Albanians, European peoples after World War II no longer nurtured large numbers of children who, on attaining adulthood, were unable to find satisfactory careers at home. Instead, when economic boom set in during the 1950s, migration started to run in an opposite direction, bringing millions of Moslems into the old heartlands of European civilization. As a result, Pakistanis in Britain, Algerians in France, Turks in West Germany, and several different ethnic strands of Central Asian and Caucasus Moslems in the Soviet Union began to staff the unattractive jobs in each country.

It is interesting to observe how the ancient nations of Europe thus came to resemble overseas lands of settlement more closely than before. For since World War II the principal cities of Europe have become polyethnic, just like American, Australian, and South African cities. The gap between center and periphery thereby narrowed still more. But this time the gap was closed not by bringing the peripheral lands nearer to European norms, but by altering the social pattern of Europe itself.

Such a reversal surely attests to the completion of a process of European expansion that dominated the world for about four and a half centuries after 1500. We now can say that the movement outward from Europe of peoples, institutions, skills, and ideas which generated the Great Frontier seems finally to have come to a halt. What new movements may take its place, time will tell. It would be naive to suppose that changes in the terms of encounter among the major branches of humanity have finally achieved a lasting equilibrium. On the contrary, flux and reflux seem likely to intensify as communications become ever denser and transport capacity expands. But the drastically one-sided character of cultural encounter that prevailed across the Great Frontier seems unlikely to recur. Only some apocalyptic disaster leading to the sudden depopulation of large parts of the earth could reproduce the frontier circumstances of the recent past.

We can discern a natural succession for the repair of the demographic catastrophe that beset disease-vulnerable populations in early modern times. European pioneering was the principal expression of that process. Each successive stage of frontier life, as analyzed nearly a century ago by Turner, established greater social complexity and a more subtly graded social hierarchy, thereby repairing the initial rent in the human occupancy of the earth.

Idealization of one or another of the stages of development toward a more fully civilized condition is a kind of romantic delusion to which both Turner and Webb, along with a large segment of the American public, were susceptible.[28] But by now the United States has come fully abreast of the old centers of European civilization in most respects. It is time our historiography caught up, and ceased to glorify a parochial past, recognizing instead our place in the grand epos of European civilization, and of the whole human adventure on earth.

This, it seems to me, is the beginning of wisdom. To put

our country back into the world from which, in truth, it never departed, even in the most isolationist decades of the nineteenth century, is the most urgent task before historians in the United States. Perhaps these lectures may provoke others to make the attempt, in order to improve details and correct the perspectives I have been able to bring to the task.

PART II

The Human Condition

AN ECOLOGICAL AND HISTORICAL VIEW

Acknowledgments

A UNIVERSITY promotes scholarship less through the leisure it confers upon faculty and students than through the routines of classroom performance that require student and teacher to have something to say at a fixed point in time, ready or not. By compelling initial formulations of a given subject matter in this way, ideas are literally forced into existence, to wither or flourish under subsequent examination as the case may be.

The Bland-Lee lectures at Clark University partake of this tradition. The lecturer is free to choose his theme but has to have something to say at the appointed time, however incomplete his research or however imperfect his preparation. Without that compulsion, this essay would never have been written.

The text as actually delivered in September 1978 has been subsequently revised and (slightly) expanded, largely in response to criticisms and suggestions coming from friends and colleagues who read the first draft. The most helpful of these include Robert McC. Adams, Albert O. Hirschman, Arcadius Kahan, Donald McCloskey, Daniel Pipes, Hugh Scogin, and Edward Tenner. Although I have not always accepted their advice nor explored all the paths they recommended to me, the balance and (I trust) the persuasiveness of the essay that follows has been significantly improved thanks to their suggestions. Nevertheless, I thought it best to stick to the main lines of argument and assertion presented on the occasion itself, since anything else would distort the record and might, by multiplying examples and modifying generalizations to take fuller account of historical complexity, actually deprive the exercise of most of its value as a conspectus of the human past.

I owe a special debt to Professor George Billias who, as

chairman of the Department of History at Clark University, acted as my host in Worcester, and to Professor Theodore von Laue who provoked the invitation in the first place, and reacted to what I had to say both sensitively and perceptively.

Chicago, 12 October 1979

MICROPARASITISM, MACROPARASITISM, AND THE URBAN TRANSMUTATION

ALTHOUGH IT IS absurd to try to distill the human adventure on earth into the narrow space of two lectures, I propose to do just that. The absurd, after all, pushes us beyond the borders of ordinary discourse; and any intellectual discipline—not least history—needs every so often to examine the framework of understanding within which detailed researches and ordinary teaching are conducted. By trying to look at all of the human past in an exceedingly narrow compass, we will be forced to think about the really major landmarks—to consider, so to speak, the geological structures underlying details of the historical landscape. Even if my notions fail to persuade you, still this adventure into rash generalization may make you more conscious of how small-scale historical knowledge fits into, and derives part of its meaning from, the overall picture we have inherited from our forerunners.

.   .   .

THE traditional framework within which the human adventure on earth has been studied in my lifetime has been about as follows. The human past fell into two main segments: prehistory and history, with the invention of writing marking the boundary. Prehistory divided into the Old Stone Age and the New Stone Age, followed by the Chalcolithic, Bronze, and Iron ages; history in turn passed through ancient, medieval, and modern periods.

On the face of things, this is a strangely discordant set of terms to apply to our past. Prehistoric periodization depended on the survival of materials from which tools and weapons were made—blithely leaving out the wood and other perishables that must have constituted a large part of the actual tool kit. On the other hand, the tripartite division of history rested originally on a very refined literary taste, being the invention of Italian humanists who believed they had inaugurated the modern age by reviving Ciceronian Latin and who deplored and defined the Middle Ages as a time when correct Latin had been forgotten.

To be sure, other meanings were subsequently poured into both classification systems. In the 1940s, V. Gordon Childe, for example, asked what uses defined ancient tool shapes and materials, and thus produced a quasi-Marxist evolution from hunting and gathering (Old Stone Age), to food producing (New Stone Age), to the urban age (Bronze Age and the entire historic period that followed).

Being older, the Italian humanists' division of history between medieval and modern has experienced rather more variegated and drastic reinterpretation. Early in the nineteenth century, for example, Leopold von Ranke organized the epochs of history in terms of interstate relations. Hence the Medieval Age began when the Roman Empire fell, and modern times started in 1494 when trans-Alpine powers eclipsed the effective sovereignty of the Italian city states. English learning usually preferred to pin modernity upon the European oceanic discoveries (1492 and all that), whereas the prophetic vision of Karl Marx defined ancient, medieval, and modern in terms of prevalent forms of labor—slave, serf, and wage.

More recently, subsections within modern times have begun to assume greater importance for many historians, eclipsing or threatening to eclipse the older tripartite division of history. This elaboration got under way in the 1880s when Arnold

Toynbee, uncle of the more famous Arnold J. Toynbee, invented the Industrial Revolution. It neatly coincided with the reign of King George III (1760-1820) for the simple reason that Toynbee had been hired at Oxford to teach a course about the history of that reign. Subsequently, other historians discovered a commercial revolution of the sixteenth century, and Fernand Braudel relocated it in the seventeenth century by emphasizing the geographic shift from Mediterranean to northern economic primacy in Europe in the 1630s. Simultaneously, and perhaps in imitation of the prehistorians, a multiplicity of technological eras have begun to decorate the pages of economic historians—the age of coal and iron, of electricity and chemicals, of atomic reactors and electronics, et cetera.

More recently, in the 1960s, it became fashionable to assert that contemporary conditions were so unprecedented that historical experience had become irrelevant. For such minds, various typologies setting up antitheses between traditional and modern societies justified a brisk dismissal of the premodern human past from any further consideration. Since they usually located the horizon of modernity in the nineteenth or twentieth centuries, the great majority of humanity's historical experience was excluded from these efforts to understand our own age.

Needless to say, I deplore the effort to dissociate humanity's deeper past from the contemporary encounter with the world. Yet a usable past must be intelligible; and it seems clear, even from my hasty remarks here, that we suffer from much confusion when it comes to any general mapping of the human condition through time. These lectures will add to the confusion by attempting to bring ecological ideas and terminology to bear. More specifically, I propose to look for shifting patterns of microparasitism and macroparasitism, treating them as twin variables that profoundly affected and continue to affect human life.

What I mean by microparasitism is, I hope, familiar enough already. The term refers to the metabolic activities of minute organisms that compete with human beings for food. They do so partly by invading the tissues of things we eat. By getting there first, microparasites can obviously forestall human efforts to capture energy from that food. Wheat rusts, animal murrains, and, more loosely, the depredations of insects and rats in human storehouses are instances of this kind of microparasitism.

Organisms can also invade human bodies and feed upon our tissues directly. Sometimes such invasions produce no obvious ill effect; often, however, sickness or death result. The impact of lethal and debilitating disease on human numbers, vigor, and ideas about the nature of things has been considerable. Encounters with microparasites—varying from individual to individual, from time to time, and from place to place in quite drastic fashion—constitute an ever present fact of biological life. Microparasitism, in short, constituted and continues to constitute a sort of nether millstone, perpetually abrading human efforts to assure individual and collective survival.

My use of the term macroparasitism, is, I must confess, less straightforward. From the time when our remote ancestors became the most formidable hunters on the face of the earth, no other species has been capable of feeding regularly upon human bodies by killing and eating them. Yet this is the ordinary meaning of the word macroparasitism; and in its proper definition, therefore, macroparasitism has played a trivial role throughout all human history.

Yet there is a metaphorical sense, it seems to me, in which one may say that when one man or group of men seize goods or compel services from other human beings, they are acting as an alien macroparasitic species acts, and they may therefore be called macroparasites by analogy. Certainly, most peasants who see someone else eat what they have produced or find themselves conscripted to work for another's benefit find that access to resources required for their own personal well-being has been reduced in proportion to the quantity of goods and services transferred by such transactions. When armed raiders break in upon a village of farmers, resemblance to the macroparasitism of one animal species on another is obvious enough. When it is tax or rent collectors who come to seize their share of the harvest, the resemblance is less obvious, since sudden death is not normally at stake in such situations. Still, if one thinks not of individuals but of biological populations, the dependence of a macroparasite on the survival of the plants or animals whose tissues it eats is similar to the dependence of the tax and rent consumer on the survival of tax and rent payers. Accordingly, customs and institutions that regulate the amount of tax and rent payments so as to allow the survival of the payers are analogous to the balances of nature that keep predators relatively few and their prey comparatively numerous—as, for instance, is true of lions and antelopes in the African game reserves.

I propose, therefore, to use the term macroparasitism to apply to exploitative relations among groups and classes of human beings. By doing so I think I will not do too much injustice to the exact ecological meaning of the word. Such a metaphorical usage has the advantage of inviting us to focus attention upon the human majority through time: those who after the invention of food production labored in the fields and paid over part of what they harvested to others who used such income for their own purposes. Only occasionally was there any palpable return to the tax and rent payer. On the other hand, protection from more ruthless, less experienced, alternative exploiters often did constitute an intangible though real quid pro quo.

If microparasitism may be likened to a nether millstone, grinding away at human populations through time, human-to-human macroparasitism has been almost as universal—an upper millstone, pressing heavily upon the majority of the human race. Between them, the two forms of parasitism usually tended to keep the peasant majority of civilized populations close to bare subsistence by systematically withdrawing resources from their control.

Though this may have been true on the average and over long enough periods of time, vast and destructive perturbations of macroparasitic-microparasitic balances often took place. Wars, epidemics, and mass migrations, which play so conspicuous a part in recorded history, amply attest to the precariousness of the ecological balances within which humanity has so far contrived to survive and even to flourish. For, despite all the catastrophes, human labor usually sufficed to repair the damage wrought by war and epidemic within a few generations. A pattern of unceasing fluctuation around an equilibrium point resulted. In principle (though not in practice) such a fluctuating equilibrium might endure for hundreds or even thousands of centuries, just as ecological equilibria do for other animals and plants.

To be sure, over a long enough time span, organic evolution alters plant and animal ecological relationships. On the foreshortened historical time scale, humanity's capacity to make discoveries and inventions does the same by sporadically tapping new forms of wealth. One invention is likely to provoke others. In that case, runaway change, echoing and reechoing within disturbed social and biological equilibria, may upset the balance between hosts and parasites for centuries at a time. In this way, human numbers and skills have repeatedly crossed previously unattainable thresholds. But always in the deeper past, a discernible tendency towards stabilization within new limits seems recognizable as macroparasitic-microparasitic balances reasserted their capacity to restrict and restrain human existence. Perhaps in a long enough time perspective, the industrial expansion of recent centuries will also conform to this pattern. New wealth, however abundant it seems, may not suffice to annul parasitism in human relations, despite what democratic theories of equality assume will, or ought to be, the case.

Yet however plausible this dismal view of the human condition may be, I do not mean to assert that it is a self-evident fact of life. On the contrary, mutuality is also a reality among human beings, and trade relationships, whereby both parties gain tangible advantage from the transaction, are as much a part of the historic record as are exploitation and lopsided taking. To be sure, trade and market-regulated production seem to have been of limited importance in the early stages of civilized history. For centuries, exchanges of goods and services, which were freely and willingly entered into by the parties concerned, flickered on and off, being perpetually liable to forcible interruption. Raiders from afar and rulers close at hand were both perennially tempted to confiscate rather than to buy; and when they confiscated, trade relations and voluntary production for market sale weakened or even disappeared entirely for a while. But market behavior always tended to take root anew because of the mutual advantages inherent in exchange of goods coming from diverse parts of the earth or produced by diversely skilled individuals. Little by little the scale and importance of mutually advantageous trade and manufacture for sale at freely negotiated prices increased. Thereby the direct clash of interest between exploited and exploiter was muted and sometimes even transcended.

How completely macroparasitic exploitation can be checked in the future seems to me an open question. So is the related question of how completely human skills can banish infectious disease or defeat rival forms of life that feed on human foods. Enormous and unexpected changes in these balances have occurred in the past; it is unlikely that infrangible limits in either direction will be attained in our time. Whatever catastrophes may lie ahead, the processes that have given humankind dominion over the face of the earth are not at an end, even if the two millstones of micro- and macroparasitism continue to grind. To identify times and occasions when systematic changes in these balances occurred will be the aim of these lectures.

.　.　.

I SUPPOSE that the first landmark of human ecological history was the advance of our remotest ancestors to the apex of the food chain. This was almost surely a result of the acquisition of language and of the superior coordination of human behavior that language allowed. Knowledge and skill could begin to accumulate when words allowed more precise discrimination of meaningful aspects of the natural environment, whether food or foe, tool or toy. No less important was the possibility of more exact cooperation in the hunt by agreeing on a plan ahead of time. Language also enormously facilitated the transmission of any useful new discovery or invention to subsequent generations. In the long run, accumulation of skills and knowledge that resulted from this capacity transformed humanity's place in the natural order.

The first fully human hunters and gatherers found themselves living in tropical Africa, surrounded by a very tight web of life. Africa's ecology included (and continues to include) a dense array of microparasites that had evolved with humanity itself. They were so adjusted to the human presence that any notable increase in human numbers promptly provoked a sharp intensification of infection and infestation.[1] Together with limitations on the availability of food, tropical microparasites sufficed to keep our remote ancestors relatively rare in the balance of nature.

The next landmark is no less a matter of speculative reconstruction, for it involved human penetration of colder and dryer zones of the earth, where most of the microparasites that limit human life in sub-Saharan Africa could not survive. Here the key invention was the use of clothes to maintain a tropical microenvironment next to the almost hairless skin we all inherit from our cradleland. A bearskin on the back, together with the domestication of fire—a skill acquired close to human beginnings—allowed survival in freezing temperatures; and when sewing and tailoring were invented to improve the fit between animal furs and the human frame, even Arctic lands became penetrable by ancient hunters. This allowed a rapid expansion of human populations around the globe.

A few microparasites probably accompanied humanity in its grand dispersal: yaws, for example, could pass from skin to skin without ever leaving the warmth of the human body. But most tropical microorganisms could not fend off lethal cold as humans had learned to do. Hunting and gathering bands that penetrated temperate zones therefore left behind nearly all of the microorganisms that kept human numbers in balance with other forms of life in the African cradleland.

Humanity's first global population boom presumably ensued, wreaking serious disturbance to pre-existing ecological balances among large-bodied animals in temperate and sub-Arctic lands and throughout the New World. Skilled hunters able to penetrate new regions of the earth must have had an easy time killing large and unwary game animals—at least to begin with. Some scholars believe that the Pleistocene disappearance of hundreds of species of such animals, especially in the Americas, was due to reckless overkill by newly arrived human hunting bands whose numbers were no longer adequately restrained by tropical microparasites.[2]

Whether or not human hunters were the principal agents in the destruction of woolly mammoths and scores of other big animals, it seems clear that as these creatures disappeared, human communities accustomed to feeding upon them faced a severe crises. It was met by intensified gathering—for example, by resort to the collection of shellfish along tidal shores, as is attested by some impressive shell middens in Europe. In several different parts of the earth, however, intensified gathering changed over into food production. Human beings learned ways of altering natural landscapes by deliberate action so as to increase the area in which a given food plant could grow. Whenever and wherever such actions became successful enough to provide a major part of the year's nutrition, a new way of life set in.

Methods of cultivation and the species of food plants human communities came to depend upon varied greatly. But the general idea of increasing the supply of food by altering natural landscapes, holding back weeds (i.e., competing plants without food value to humans), and increasing the abundance of a few desired kinds of plants was everywhere the same. It seems also to be true that efforts along these lines began at approximately the same time, even though results were sometimes delayed, as in the Americas, where far-reaching changes in the genetics of maize were required before the new patterns of cultivation could produce really large amounts of human food.

Whenever human beings succeeded in establishing a productive form of agriculture (with or without domestication of animals), the increase in population and the change in habit of life that food production brought with it increased the importance of microparasitism. Human actions aimed at producing a uniform stand of a single kind of plant offered an enlarged scope to all the insects, fungi, and viruses that were natural parasites of the plant in question. Thus, the more successful human farmers were in establishing a uniform plant population in their fields, the more vulnerable they became to losses from infections of this kind. In addition, food harvested and stored for use throughout the year became vulnerable to another array of parasites: rats and mice, insects, molds, and the like.

But humans could see their animal and insect competitors. Intelligence then often circumvented disaster, for example, by discovering ways to make storage jars proof against insects and mice. Even fungi and viruses could sometimes be fended off. Conditions of moisture and temperature conducive to the propagation of such forms of life could be—at least sometimes—both observed and subsequently avoided or minimized by appropriate human actions. But every deliberate alteration of natural life balances required a never-ending battle against "weed" species, ever ready to compete with human consumers, as parasites upon the plants that human actions had made abnormally abundant in the balance of nature.

Parallel to this intensified struggle against competitors for the food humans hoped to consume themselves was an intensification of infections within human bodies. Communities that remained in the same location for years on end became vulnerable to a cluster of infections that enter the human body through the mouth and are excreted with the faeces. Hunters perpetually on the move are seldom exposed to the anal-oral path of infection, while villagers living in proximity to their own faeces year after year become fair game for dysenteries and the like that are propagated from host to host in this way. The drinking of contaminated water was, after all, an everyday practice until 130 years ago, because human senses, unaided by the microscope, could not detect bacterial contamination.

[79]

The shift to food production permitted a second surge in human population, since a landscape given over to grain fields can support many times as many human beings as the same landscape used only for hunting and the gathering of wild foods. Still, there were limits to the amount of land that could be made into fields in every case, and before long the restraining force of intensified microparasitism also made itself felt. In the Near East, where information about the transition to food production is far greater than elsewhere, a leveling off in population density seems to have set in within two or three millennia of the first beginnings of agriculture. Frontier villages continued to multiply as farmers penetrated new regions as far afield as North Africa, Europe, and India. But in the initial heartland of the Near East, after about 5000 B.C. a potentially stable adaptation for humanity in its newly won ecological niche as engineer of the plant kingdom may plausibly be discerned from what remains a sketchy archaeological sampling of neolithic village sites. In other parts of the earth, too little is known to suggest a similar rhythm of initial expansion and subsequent stabilization of skills and numbers, though on a priori grounds it seems probable.

Nevertheless, the earliest village pattern of agriculture did not endure indefinitely. In the sixth millennium B.C., new and much more productive patterns of cultivation were inaugurated along the banks of streams flowing into the Tigris-Euphrates River. Two inventions were critical: irrigation, which brought water to growing crops as needed, thus assuring heavy yields; and the plow, which allowed field workers to keep at least four times as much land in tillage as was possible when only human muscles had been harnessed to the task. Plowing also made permanent cultivation of the same fields possible. Weeds could be controlled by fallowing, that is, by the practice of leaving some fields empty in order to destroy weeds by plowing the land during the growing season. Killing off competing species in this way created an ecological vacuum and did so easily and cheaply. In the next year, grain sown in such ground yielded abundant harvests, especially if the area was also watered artificially. Disasters were not completely banished: rust or blight on the grain or a flood to destroy the growing crop was still possible. But that sort of thing was unusual. In most years, the harvest richly rewarded the effort expended in its production.

Thus, by keeping twice as much land under the plow as was needed for the year's food, and by seeding only half of this land each season, a fully sessile agriculture arose in the Tigris-Euphrates valley, whereas in earlier times the only way neolithic cultivators had been able to escape weed infestation had been to abandon old fields after a few years' cultivation and carve new ones from the forest by the technique known as slash and burn. Plowing and irrigation obviously allowed far more intensive agricultural use of land than slash and burn cultivation had done. On the other hand, the gain carried its own nemesis, for fully sessile agricultural villages were also liable to new and intensified forms of parasitism.

Consider macroparasitism first. The fact that farmers could count on regular and abundant harvests made them capable of supporting others than themselves, if those others could find a way of persuading or compelling them to hand over part of their harvest. This did indeed occur between 4000 and 3000 B.C. in the Tigris-Euphrates flood plain. With the definition of customary patterns for transferring food from those who produced it to persons who no longer had to till the ground in order to eat, new sorts of social diversity became possible. Skills could accumulate as full-time specialists devoted their ingenuity to old and new tasks. The resultant highly skilled societies we commonly call civilized to distinguish them from simpler, more uniform human communities. Cities, where specialized elites clustered, were the hallmark of civilization.

No doubt, if tax and rent collectors pressed too heavily on those who worked in the fields, the option of flight remained. But in practice this was a costly alternative. It was rare indeed that a fleeing farmer could expect to find a place where he could raise a crop in the next season, starting from raw land. And to go without food other than what could be found in the wild for a whole year was impractical. Hence the high yield and dependability of irrigation plowing tied farmers to the land quite effectually and made such populations easy targets for tax and rent collectors. Civilization and the differentiation of occupational skills and routines that characterizes civilization depended on this elementary fact. And human society in its civilized form came to be fundamentally divided between hosts (the food producers) and parasites (those who ate without themselves working in the fields).

To be sure, it is not clear that the new relationship was especially burdensome to food producers at first. As long as a regular routine of work in the fields produced a surplus of grain over and above what the cultivator and his family could themselves consume in the course of the year, to part with the unneeded portion was no great loss. In return, the priests who managed the earliest irrigation societies assured good relations with the gods—no small matter, after all, in a world in which divine displeasure could bring swift disaster in the form of devastating floods or some other natural catastrophe. The planning and building of new irrigation projects and other public works—temples primarily—also fell under the jurisdiction of priestly managers and, when skillfully carried through, added to the total wealth and splendor of the society in a direct and obvious way. Hence the initial relationship between food producers and food consumers may have been symbiotic, involving relatively little loss to the peasant majority. But the statistical facts that would support or contradict this hypothesis are irrecoverable, and it is also possible that harsher exploitative relationships asserted themselves from the very beginning of civilized history.

Three aspects of this third major mutation of human life patterns seem worth comment here. First, the occupational specialization that permitted the rapid elaboration of skills thereby intensified the ecological upheaval that human actions imposed upon the natural web of life. From its inception, civilization acted upon its environment, altering and changing what had been there before in accord with the will of an increasingly skilled, powerful, and numerous population in the fertile plains. For example, timber, building stone, metals, and a long list of rare and precious commodities could only be found at a distance from the river flood plains, where the rich alluvium covered the subsoil and the climate would not allow large trees to grow. To bring such commodities from afar required improvements in transportation: wheeled vehicles, sailing ships, and the human organization needed to cut, quarry, or in other ways prepare and then transport goods across hundreds of miles. This meant that the civilization of the flood plains disturbed preexisting ecological patterns far and wide, imposing, or seeking to impose, complementary though often sharply contrasting patterns of behavior on peoples round about.

This side of the urban transmutation of human society is quite familiar, and I need not elaborate upon it further. A second aspect of urbanism—a marked intensification of microparasitism—is less familiar, however. Irrigation, for example, exposed cultivators to waterborne parasites, most notably the organism that completes its life cycle by moving between snails and men through fresh water, causing human schistosomiasis. Sewage and water supply problems, already significant for neolithic villagers, increased with the size of settlement, so that the anal-oral path of infection also carried an intensified traffic as cities came into being. Even more significant for the long-range future of human populations was the fact that when civilized communities achieved a sufficient size and density, viruses that pass from human to human via airborne droplets found it possible to survive indefinitely.

Such infections—smallpox, measles, whooping cough, and the like—almost certainly became human diseases by transfer from animal herd populations. When they do not kill their host, these infections provoke long-lasting immunity reactions in the bloodstream. Hence if a virus is to survive indefinitely, it must always be able to find new and previously uninfected individuals, so that the chain of virus generations will not be interrupted. Only large human populations allow this: in recent times, for example, measles required a community of over 450,000 persons in order to survive. Obviously, birthrates and the custom of sending children to school affect the way a disease like measles was propagated in our time: still, so high a figure suggests how precarious survival of these viral infections must have been initially. Clearly, such an infection could only exist on a permanent basis among civilized societies where human populations were comparatively dense and communications nets far-flung.

Adding such viral infections to intensified anal-oral infections and to those infections transmitted to human populations via alternative hosts, whether insect or otherwise, obviously increased the microparasitic burden civilized populations had to carry. In short, organic evolution was catching up with humanity, weaving a new web of life around enlarged human numbers as a substitute for the African tropical network that had once restrained human populations so effectually.

There was, however, an ironical side effect. Disease-experienced populations in densely inhabited civilized centers acquired a notable epidemiological advantage vis-à-vis isolated, disease-inexperienced peoples. When newly inaugurated, contact between civilized populations and such isolated human communities often resulted in the outbreak of massively lethal epidemics among the former isolates. The effect of such vulnerability was to break down the capacity of such communities to resist civilized encroachment. The remarkable fewness of civilizations and the relative homogeneity of massive civilized populations in such places as China, the Middle East, and Europe resulted in large measure from this epidemiological-sociological process—or so I argue in my book, *Plagues and Peoples*,[3] to which I refer you for a fuller development of this line of thought.

The third aspect of the urban transmutation to which I wish to draw attention is the metamorphosis of macroparasitism that accompanied occupational specialization. Soon after cities first arose, the new skills that were generated by specialization and the relatively enormous wealth that resulted from irrigation and plowing made such cities worthwhile objects of attack by armed outsiders. Perhaps the initiation of armed aggression rested with the city folk, who probably took arms in hand when first they ventured forth to seek timber and metals and other needed goods. This, at any rate, is a plausible interpretation of what may lie behind the story of Gilgamesh as transmitted to us by much later (ca. 1800 B.C.) literary artists. But whether or not city dwellers were the first aggressors, it seems certain that during the third millennium B.C., raiding and plundering became an important feature of Mesopotamian life. Other civilizations in other parts of the earth seem also to have experienced a parallel shift from predominantly priestly to predominantly military management, whenever and wherever civilized skills created sufficient wealth to make raiding and warfare worthwhile.

Men preying upon other men thus began to create a new kind of macroparasitism, distinctive of civilization in much the same way that the viral dropletborne infections were also distinctive of civilization. Only a rich and differentiated society could sustain human-to-human macroparasitism by producing enough wealth to make its forcible seizure a viable, ongoing way of life for specialized warrior populations. Viruses could only survive when the density of human populations surpassed a critical threshold; warriors needed both a suitable number of potential subjects and a suitably advanced distribution of skills among them. Without numbers and skills, the long-term survival of a class that consumed without itself producing either the food or the arms its members required was impossible. Such a ruling class, therefore, was as much a hallmark of civilization as were the viral diseases. Poorer and more dispersed human communities simply could not sustain either form of parasite for long.

A warrior ruling class resembled viral infections in another way: a society capable of supporting their claims upon the body social became lethally formidable in contact with other, less differentiated communities. What viruses started, military specialists completed—defeating, demoralizing, and in general breaking down the autonomy and independence of border folk who, having come into contact with an expanding civilized society, ordinarily lost their separate identity as the price of survival.

Between an intensified microparasitism and this new style of civilized macroparasitism, therefore, it is safe to say that significant additional drains upon the resources available to peasant farming populations came into play during the first thousand years of Near Eastern civilized history. Clearly, the disturbance of older balances that human skills had created when the urban transmutation began was in process of correction, even though human capacity for fresh invention from time to time continued to disturb the equilibrium between civilized populations, productivity, microparasites, and macroparasites.

I do not intend to undertake the application of this scheme to the ups and downs of political and economic history in the ancient Near East or elsewhere, as this would require far larger compass than these two lectures provide. Let me merely remark, therefore, that the new exposure of human populations to micro- and macroparasitic invasions tended across time to move from sporadic epidemic to more nearly stable endemic forms. As far as microparasitic infection is concerned this is a familiar proposition. Adaptation between host and parasite always tends toward mutual accommodation, and in recent times expert observers have recorded in detail some striking examples of how accommodation proceeds when a new infection breaks in upon a previously inexperienced population.[4]

Viral herd diseases became diseases of childhood wherever human populations and communications nets attained sufficient density to maintain the infection on an enduring basis. Even though rates of lethality might remain high, human populations found it comparatively easy to replace young children who might die of smallpox or measles or other similar infections. Costs of such endemic exposure were far less than when the same disease visited a community only at long intervals—say once every thirty to fifty years—in which case every person who had been born since the infection had last been present was vulnerable. In such circumstances, death of parents and of the economically productive age groups was far more costly than an identical death rate spread evenly across time and confined to infants and young children. In such a fashion, then, infections could and did accommodate themselves to human populations, securing a more assured life cycle for the infectious organisms as well as for their human hosts. This is the way organic evolution works; and as childhood disease patterns established themselves, civilized concentrations of human populations became more securely adapted to their microparasitic environment.

A parallel evolution also occurred on the macroparasitic side. The major manifestation was the rise of imperial command structures. These became ever more elaborate and extensive from the time of the first recorded conqueror, Sargon of Akkad (ca. 2250 B.C.), to that of the Achaemenids, the Han, the Romans, and the Mauryans in the Old World, and of the Incas and Aztecs (building upon the work of their predecessors) in the New. In all parts of the civilized world, the key device facilitating the rise and consolidation of these imperial command structures was acceptance of the bureaucratic principle. By this I mean the way in which an individual appointed to office through some ritual act assumed a role that changed his behavior and that of persons around him in far-reaching and more or less predictable ways. Behavior changed because such an appointed official became a symbol of the sovereign ruler himself. In this way, sovereignty could be exercised at a distance and in the absence of the ruler, as long as officials and those around them accepted the roles that appointment (and replacement of one officeholder by another) implied.

Once government at a distance became feasible in this fashion, more stable patterns of contact between rulers and ruled made long-range advantage more apparent, while short-range considerations became less compelling than before. To put things in a nutshell: from the ruler's point of view, plunder became less attractive than taxes, and from the subject's side, a predictable tax payment became preferable to the enhanced risk of depredation that freedom from taxes and the absence of a powerful protector entailed.

The consequent accommodation between ruler and ruled

was very like the accommodation between microparasite and host that endemic disease establishes. Custom and institutional forms defined an acceptable level of rent and tax payments—acceptable in the sense that in most years, when weather was normal and no external disaster intervened, customary levies were compatible with the survival of the tax and rent payers until the next season. One can, indeed, think of the relationship as a sticky market in protection costs. Too high a price for protection either killed off the tax and rent payers by leaving them too little for their own sustenance or persuaded them to flee to some other place where lower protection costs promised an easier life. On the other hand, too low a price for protection might allow an outside challenger to raid and plunder because the resources at the disposal of the imperial officials and military establishment were inadequate to drive intruders from the scene.

To be sure, there were enormous inefficiencies in all of the imperial command structures whose details are known to historians. In particular, local magnates and landholders commonly intercepted income from cultivators and weakened the power of central authorities by diverting resources to their own uses—only part of which were related to the protection of the rent payers. Yet feudal devolution of this kind was restrained by the fact that every civilized society confronted external rivals. In Eurasia, the most notable such rivals were bands of steppe cavalrymen, whose nomadic way of life fitted them for war and whose mobility allowed them to take advantage of any weakening of local defenses on the part of civilized rulers. Most of Eurasian political history, in fact, can be viewed as an unending fluctuation between imperial consolidation and feudal devolution, punctuated from time to time by epidemics of nomad invasion whenever the defenses of settled agricultural communities became insufficient to hold back armed raiders from the steppe.

The macroparasitic process, in other words, tended to seek an equilibrium point at which tax and rent payments transferred to the ruling classes sustained an armed establishment capable of repelling outside raiders, yet not so large as to require or permit its members to resort to plunder and rapine on their own account at the expense of the peasantry and of customary, constituted rent and tax collectors. When the optimal point was approximated, security of life for the producers and income for the rulers could both be maximized. But defining that optimum and maintaining it when defined was difficult indeed. Rulers and landowners were systematically advantaged by having superior force at their disposal. Countervailing this lopsidedness was the weight of custom, reinforced by religiously sanctioned general rules.

By a process of trial and error, perpetual interplay between armed force and the force of custom and religious injunction defined effective limits to rent and tax collection at a point that gave the producers a modest cushion against a year of bad crops. Only in this way could they survive the kinds of natural disasters that constantly afflicted farming communities. In a good year, surpluses retained in peasant hands could be converted into capital goods: tools, draught animals, clothing. In a bad year, cultivators often reached the verge of starvation, or died of hunger, in which case decades might pass before human numbers could recover.

Yet however important war and taxes may have been for civilized populations subjected to imperial command structures, epidemic disease was probably more important in cutting back population and wealth. This was, at any rate, true in the centuries and regions of the earth where approximate data can be found—that is, in early modern Europe and China. Yet even in the absence of quantifiable data, it seems certain that sporadic exposure to lethal diseases was very old among rural populations in contact with and subject to urban centers. Scattered populations in the hinterland could not sustain the endemic viral diseases of civilization. Instead they became liable to peaks of infection and heavy, abrupt die-off after years had passed without exposure to the disease in question, that is, after a long enough time for a sufficient number of vulnerable people to come into existence to support a new epidemic.

. . .

OBVIOUSLY stability was never fully achieved, either in microparasitic or macroparasitic balances. Yet it seems plausible to suggest that shortly before the Christian era the kind of approximation to a stable state that I imputed to neolithic villagers before the rise of cities in the Near East can be detected within each of the civilizations that had sprung into existence in Eurasia by that time. The rise of the Roman and Han empires west and east was matched by the existence of comparable, if less well-known, imperial structures in the regions in between—in Mesopotamia, Iran, and India.

One can imagine this as constituting a sort of natural climax and end point of adaptations arising from the shift to agriculture as the principal basis of human existence. Increased human numbers, which food production occasioned, had found appropriate patterns of social organization, and the enlarged scope for micro- and macroparasitism had set limits to the further growth of human populations. Only along undeveloped frontiers—in southern China and India, or across the Eurasian steppe to the north, and in the forested zones of northwest Europe—was there much prospect for expansion. Each of these regions offered obstacles to agricultural settlement. The obstacles were partly climatic and technical. Plowing the steppe was a formidable task for light scratch plows, which were all that

[91]

existed at that time, and northwest Europe was too wet for Mediterranean farming methods to work. In addition, epidemiological obstacles were also important, since south China, Southeast Asia, and south India, together with all of sub-Saharan Africa, were infested with malarial and other parasites that made dense human occupation precarious, at least until such time as human labor was able to transform natural landscapes by improved drainage and the like so as to reduce exposure.

Yet even if such a hypothesis seems logically attractive, the path of historical development actually proved it false. What happened instead was that new patterns of human interaction began to affect societies and civilizations as transport and communication across Asia and the southern oceans assumed regular, organized forms. This became important from about the time of the Christian era, when caravans started to travel from China to Syria and back again, while ships connected Egypt with India and India with China through a series of segmented voyages.

A multitude of customary and technical breakthroughs were necessary to sustain this sort of long distance transport of men and goods. How to build and pay for a ship was only the beginning. Navigational know-how, crew discipline, security of passengers and their goods on board and in the ports along the way all had to achieve satisfactory definitions. For caravans, the rules of the road were at least as complicated. Safety lay in numbers, but keeping scores or hundreds of beasts of burden moving at the same pace for thousands of miles was no easy matter, especially since they had to be fed almost every day and if they carried their own fodder, useful payloads quickly diminished to the vanishing point.

Protection from robbers along the way was, of course, crucial both for ships and caravans. Indeed, long distance trade on a regular basis became possible only when constituted authorities en route all agreed that it was advantageous to allow goods and merchants to pass through territory they controlled, paying such fees for safe passage as the traffic would bear. Trade tolls could allow rulers access to a trickle (or even to a torrent) of wealth otherwise unattainable to them; but it took a long time for the possibilities of this sort of parasitism on commerce to become apparent, since everything depended on the scale of the transactions taking place. In the short run, high tolls—even outright confiscation—brought greater gain to local rulers. But, paradoxically, lower tolls might produce a larger total income by attracting more business. Finding an optimal level for assessing tolls on trade was presumably a matter of trial and error. The process must have worked in much the same way that customary rates for rent and tax collection set tolerable burdens upon local peasantries throughout the civilized world.

About the time of the Christian era, these technical, political, and sociological adjustments had attained such a degree of perfection as to allow long-distance trade to assume a new importance in human affairs. All the great civilizations of Eurasia came to be regularly connected with each other by shipping and by animal pack trains, and an expanded range of trade probes went out from civilized centers into barbarian lands that lay both north and south of the slender belt of dense agricultural settlement to which civilized forms of society were still confined.

Human historical relationships thereby began to assume a new scale—ecumenical rather than civilizational in scope. I would like to call the shift a "commercial transmutation," and treat its course and consequences as analogous to the urban transmutation that inaugurated the rise of civilizations. The urban transmutation of human society had begun between 4000 and 3000 B.C. and, as we have just seen, matured into imperial bureaucratic states and what I have termed "civilized" patterns of infection by about 1 B.C. The commercial transmutation, being a mere two thousand years old, has yet to arrive at any comparable climax equilibrium. It is unlikely to do so until some kind of world government emerges, for only a government extending completely around the globe seems capable of matching the commercial exchanges that have become so massive and important to everyday living in recent centuries.

Although human adjustments to the commercial transmutation are not yet complete, we can still hope to analyze its initial stages with the same broad brush I have used in discussing the impact of the urban transmutation that preceded it.

The first point that emerges from such a consideration is this: the initial impact of the commercial transmutation was epidemiologically disastrous, at least for the two extremes of the ecumene, Rome and China. Previously separate civilized disease pools flowed together. Viruses and other infectious organisms moved with ships and caravans across previously uncrossable distances. Relatively dense, previously unexposed populations thus became vulnerable to lethal infection on a hitherto unprecedented scale.

The result was registered in the Mediterranean world by the so-called Antonine plagues of the second century A.D. when, perhaps, measles and smallpox first broke in upon the population of the Roman empire. Drastic depopulation (up to one-third at first onset) and corresponding impoverishment ensued. Eventually, as one disease disaster followed another, the military, bureaucratic, and *rentier* drain upon the productive classes of the Mediterranean became insupportable, and the Roman empire disintegrated under barbarian pressure and internal disorganization. Very similar events occurred in China, where the Han empire also collapsed in the third century A.D., allowing barbarians to invade a depopulated landscape.

In the Middle Eastern lands and in India, no comparably drastic die-off from disease seems to have occurred, although records from those parts of the world are less well-preserved and have been less thoroughly studied than is the case for Rome and China. Imperial bureaucratic consolidation of those regions had been more precarious before the Christian era than at the extremes of the civilized world, perhaps because micro-parasitic burdens on the population were greater and allowed a smaller amount of resources to be concentrated in the hands of rulers and landlords.

Whether or not that was the case, the setback to wealth, population, and imperial bureaucratic administration that occurred in China and the Mediterranean lands inaugurated a thousand years of large-scale instability all across the Eurasian civilized world. To be sure, the initial disease disasters that arose from intensified travel across the breadth of the continent were in time counteracted by the diffusion of superior ideas and techniques that added to human wealth and power and probably also helped to stabilize civilized society. These travelled along the same paths as disease germs did, sometimes arriving sooner, sometimes taking root only later.

The most obvious instance of this process was the rise and dissemination of the great world religions—Christianity, Buddhism, Islam, and Hinduism—as well as of less numerically successful rivals—Judaism, Manichaeism, and Zoroastrianism. Astrological and alchemical ideas also spread widely; so did devices like stirrups, wind and water mills, the abacus, and place notation for numbers. Religions of salvation clearly made life on earth more endurable for their adherents and sometimes may have cushioned collisions within society—insofar at least as the ethical prescriptions of the respective religions were able to modify and mollify human behavior. In this sense, their rise and spread was as useful to civilized society as was the propa-

[95]

gation of water mills, horse collars, sternpost rudders, or any of the other superior techniques that originated or diffused more widely during the European Dark Ages.

At the same time, one must also admit that the appearance and spread of religions that commanded intense human loyalties and channeled aspirations toward a supernal realm introduced a new, or newly powerful, focus for human conflict as well. The righteousness with which Christians fought Moslems and with which Moslems attacked Hindu idolaters is too familiar to need emphasis here. Religious conviction embittered such collisions and probably made them more blood-spattered than would otherwise have been the case. Moreover, within a single society, when differences of opinion about salvation surged to the fore, civil strife was sometimes intensified by the belief that eternal salvation and damnation were at stake. This was true within Christendom, as the wars of the Reformation attest; it was equally true within Islam, as struggles between Shi'a and Sunni prove. Among Buddhists and Confucians, doctrinal differences never inspired comparable conflicts, although armed monks and angry Confucians sometimes did resort to military force in domestic broils.

Yet even though religions of salvation inspired or embittered some human conflicts in this fashion, it is arguable that for most of the people most of the time, the moral injunctions and the hope for a better future that the teachings of the higher religions inculcated conduced to survival. Had this not been the case, the new religions surely would not have spread and survived as they did.

More generally, it seems clear to me that all human ideas and techniques faced an intensified selection for their utility under the disturbed political-social conditions that the disease disasters of the first Christian centuries inaugurated; and by about the year 1000 A.D., one can perhaps assume that the resulting enhancement of civilized capacities—both for social order and productivity within, and for defense without (epidemiological as well as military)—had laid the groundwork for a new upsurge of wealth and power that slowly became manifest across the entire breadth of the Eurasian ecumene.

Prior to that time, two rival and not very well-reconciled principles struggled for control over the civilized populations of Eurasia. On the one hand, there was the command system of empire, capable of mobilizing goods and manpower for vast projects, whether of peace or war. On the other hand, there was the price system, capable also of mobilizing human and material resources as long as superior force was not brought to bear in such a way as to interrupt the exchange of goods and services. Rulers and men of the sword commonly lived in awkward symbiosis with merchants and men of the marketplace. This had been true from the beginnings of civilization; what was different in the initial stages of the commercial transmutation was that political-military power often came to depend in significant degree on materials and services supplied to the rulers by merchants who responded to pecuniary and market motives more readily and more efficiently than to bureaucratic command.

Merchants were, in fact, objects of very general disdain and moral opprobrium. Ordinary people toiling in the fields to produce a harvest year after year felt that a man who bought cheap and sold dear was fundamentally dishonest, since he added nothing to what he sold but nonetheless profited by raising its price. Most rulers concurred, even when they tolerated and protected cheating and chaffering merchants. The plain and fundamental fact was that merchants' behavior violated patterns of mutuality that prevailed within primary groupings, whether among simple village folk or amidst the grandeur of a royal court where hospitality and gift giving supplemented prowess in cementing relations between the ruler and his military followers.

To be sure, a skillful merchant could sometimes enter into the warriors' gift giving by offering precious possessions gratis to a local ruler in confident expectation of receiving even more generous gifts in return. Marco Polo, the jewel merchant, made his way across Asia in this manner; and, in general, it was in the steppe regions of Eurasia that this technique found its greatest scope. In Islamic lands, a far more stable and predictable alliance between merchants and warriors resulted from Mohammed's revelation and example. Mohammed (570-632) had been a merchant before Allah chose him as his messenger, and the city of Mecca in which he lived was an important trade center where the social leaders of the community were themselves merchants as well as warriors. Mohammed united the nomad tribesmen of Arabia with city-based merchants under the banner of his revelation, and in succeeding generations, when the "True Believers" conquered vast agricultural regions of the Middle East and North Africa, the resulting alliance between warrior and trader remained firm. Yet I do not think that distrust of merchants disappeared from Islamic lands: rather the normal, underlying peasant dislike of tax and rent collectors merged into a parallel dislike for cheating traders. Among Christians and Confucians, as is well-known, overt condemnation of greed and price gouging entered the high literary tradition; Buddhists, so far as I know, remained doctrinally indifferent, although in practice Buddhism and merchant communities came to be closely interconnected everywhere north of the Himalayas.

Despite the accommodation to merchant manners and morals that Islam and Buddhism exhibited, I would argue that the Christian and Confucian condemnation of cheating in the marketplace was closer to majority (that is, peasant) opinion. Yet however morally dubious their behavior might be, if it were given sufficient scope, merchants, acting in response to perceived self-interest and known price differentials, could assemble and assort goods and services at lower cost than any bureaucratic command system could. The market could attract goods from afar, crossing political frontiers and ocean vastnesses in ways that no ruler could hope to do on the strength of his own word of command, no matter how emphatic. Even within a single jurisdiction, men who saw their personal self-interest tied up directly in the safe delivery of a particular consignment of goods from place to place commonly performed the task more efficiently than officials who had compulsory labor at their disposal. Hence whenever rulers and military classes tolerated merchants and refrained from taxing them so heavily or robbing them so often as to inhibit trade and commerce, new potentialities of economic production arising from regional specialization and economies of scale in manufacture could begin to show their capacity to increase human wealth.

The upshot remained very much in doubt until after 1000 A.D. Distrust, disdain, and dislike of merchants often cut back or destroyed trade linkages; raiding and migrations of barbarian peoples disrupted existing command and market systems alike. Yet command and market systems continually revived and at the same time competed against one another in regulating human behavior on a mass scale. Only after the year 1000 did the balance begin to tip perceptibly and in an enduring way in favor of an enlarged scope for market-regulated behavior. With that slow change in world balances the modern age, as I propose to define it, set in.

MICROPARASITISM, MACROPARASITISM, AND THE COMMERCIAL TRANSMUTATION

In my first lecture I traced the development of humanity to its achievement of a potentially stable pattern of life under conditions of civilization. By about 1 A.D., commands issued from a sovereign center and applied locally by bureaucratic agents of a distant ruler acting in uneasy collaboration with local landlords, chieftains, and other men of power could regulate and (more or less) safeguard the sorts of mutual dependency that urban specialization had called into being among populations living hundreds of miles apart from one another. Such territorially extensive states as the Han, Roman, Parthian, Mauryan, and Kushan empires may therefore be considered as constituting an institutionally adequate response to the novelties inherent in the urban transmutation that began about 4000 B.C. in Mesopotamia.

It is noteworthy that similar state structures arose not just in the Old World but also in the New, beginning about 1000 years later. Amerindian social organization had indeed not passed beyond this level of organization at the time the Spaniards broke in upon the Aztec and Inca empires of Mexico and Peru, bringing them to an abrupt and catastrophic end. The apparent convergence of patterns of development in mutually isolated regions of the earth suggests that the evolution from priestly to military-bureaucratic management was not simply accidental. Instead it seems plausible to believe that the intensified human interdependence that had been induced by urban

[100]

specialization needed a protective carapace. Bureaucratic command systems were the simplest way to meet that need, perpetuating into adulthood a childlike dependence on a superior's direction.

My second major point was that, beginning about 1 A.D., a new kind of transformation began to assert its power over human behavior in the Old World—a change I propose to call the "commercial transmutation." This refers to an enlarged commerce that began to link China with the Mediterranean and both with India soon after the Christian era. Long-distance trade of this kind responded mainly to market price differentials. Decisions and actions initiated by thousands of private persons affected the movement of caravans and ships—and determined what they would carry.

Of course, such decisions were also affected by bureaucratic commands. Governments were always good customers—for some goods they were the only customers. But insofar as trade moved across jurisdictional boundaries, the power of officials and rulers was checked by the unwillingness of merchants to buy or sell at prices that would not meet their costs and assure them a profit as well. Official acts that violated this principle—a compulsory purchase at less than market prices or outright confiscation—dried up trade very rapidly. The same applied to more local exchanges within a single state. Thus, insofar as rulers and their officials fixed prices at less than market levels—a policy especially prevalent in the grain trade—they inhibited the development of the private sector of the economy and perpetuated the command principle whereby men acted not of their own free will but in obedience to orders coming from someone above them in the political-social hierarchy.

Civilized societies for the next thousand years exhibited an uneasy and fluctuating combination of command and market-regulated behavior, with neither principle unambiguously in the ascendant. Clearly, in times and places where the market principle was at a minimum, human beings obeyed more readily, having no obvious alternative. Yet when communication improved, for whatever reason, so that information about price differentials between here and there became available, the possibility of gain through private trading became apparent; and in proportion as that possibility was actually acted on so that mutually advantageous exchanges multiplied, resistance to unqualified obedience to official commands mounted. In such circumstances, commands continued to be effective only where they reinforced and conformed to the price patterns established by private trade relations.

Always at the bottom of society, the peasant majority continued to respond mainly to command. Rent and tax payments were imposed on them from above: price had little or nothing to do with it. To begin with, trade in agricultural products was an affair of landlords, whose rents readily exceeded their capacity to consume food, making sale in exchange for imported rarities or city-made luxuries a very attractive proposition. Town-based merchants thus found natural allies in landlords. Both classes sought to withdraw resources from the control of bureaucratic officials in order to maximize their personal well-being and standard of living.

Officials, of course, were often landlords or closely associated with landlords, with the result that the opposition was far from clear-cut or conscious. But the possibility of and temptation towards subversion of the simple marshalling of human and material resources in response to words of command was implanted like a low-grade chronic infection in the tissues of imperial bureaucratic empires thanks to merchants' and landlords' mutual interest in expanding the private market. After about 1000 A.D. this chronic infection of the constituted public order took on new virulence and by degrees penetrated more and more of the body social throughout the civilized world. In the most severely affected regions, the market even reached out to envelop the peasantry at the very bottom of society.

Before this take-off became unambiguous, local ups and downs between market and command behavior could be quite sharp. In the Mediterranean world, for example, the high point for trade and market behavior came between about 300 B.C. and 100 A.D.—stimulated, in part, by the way in which Alexander of Macedon squandered the gold hoard Persian kings had accumulated across generations. The enlarged money supply lubricated commerce; so did the rise of commercially minded Greeks to high official positions in the Hellenistic monarchies. From its Eastern Mediterranean focus, trade and market behavior slopped over into the Indian Ocean and towards the western Mediterranean as well. And this expanding commercial network provided the principle impetus for the establishment of caravan and shipping links with distant China.

In the second and third centuries A.D. came disastrous disease, and the Roman government had to revert to taxation in kind because market behavior had withered so drastically that its lubricant, ready cash, had almost disappeared and could no longer provide a practical basis for support of the army and officialdom. Yet even in the worst of times, trade did not completely come to a halt, and commercial linkages with China and India remained sporadically alive.

In ensuing centuries, rebellion from within and raiding from the steppes frequently broke up imperial command structures in the Mediterranean and all across Eurasia. But the advantages of centralization for defense tended, no less persistently, to reestablish territorially extensive states. Moreover, such states sometimes drew an important part of their resources from tolls on trade. This was especially true in the arid zones of Asia, lying between Egypt and India (Arabia, Baluchistan) and between

Mesopotamia and China (Iran, Turan, and Sinkiang). In these regions, local agricultural resources were slender, so that rents and taxes could not constitute an adequate basis of empire; trade income accordingly mattered more. Yet tolls on trade constituted a very precarious basis for state power because long-distance exchanges were persistently vulnerable to local violence anywhere along the way. Still, this type of commerce revived no less persistently whenever a modicum of public order and the policy of local rulers reduced the risks of moving precious goods to acceptable proportions.

The role of steppe nomads in this fluctuating balance was critical. They conquered settled populations repeatedly; but when they could not raid with impunity they traded instead. This was because the steppe peoples' way of life made them peculiarly susceptible to trade. Their herds did not, of themselves, provide an optimal basis for human survival. But by offering animal products in exchange for grain, nomads could secure a much enhanced food supply compared to what they could enjoy by living solely on meat and milk. Plainly, more people could survive on the steppes and in the semidesert fringe lands that lay to the south of cultivable regions of Eurasia by giving up a biologically unneeded concentration of protein in their diet and substituting cheaper carbohydrates. Trade in a wide variety of other objects—weapons, slaves, jewels, information—attached itself to this basic pattern of exchange, which was, of course, no less advantageous to landlords and city folk in agricultural regions whose diet, if restricted to cereals, was likely to be short of protein.

The result was to create a loosely interacting continuum across the Eurasian steppe and in the desert fringe lands to the south of Middle Eastern and Mediterranean centers of civilization. These vast regions where nomadism, raiding war parties, and peaceable caravans all came to coexist linked the separate civilizations of the Old World more and more closely from the time when horseback riding first imparted a new mobility to steppe and desert dwellers (ninth century B.C.). The role of nomad peoples reached a climax in the thirteenth century A.D. when the empire of Genghis Khan gave political and military expression to the increasingly intimate symbiosis between Eurasian grasslands and grain fields.

Once patterns of protein-carbohydrate exchange became firmly established so that denser steppe populations could arise, the conditions of their lives quite literally required nomads to observe customs that protected traders from intolerable exactions. Each year survival depended on getting hold of enough grain to go round. Flocks and herds could carry themselves to market, but grain coming back had to move by caravan. Nomads thus readily occupied part of their time as caravan personnel, being already familiar with the management of animals. Moving back and forth between their homelands in steppe and desert, on the one hand, and civilized centers of life, on the other, such personnel became thoroughly exposed to merchants' ideas and values. Familiarity with the charms of civilization therefore infiltrated the nomad world, bearing a thoroughly commercial tinge. Although Arabia in the age of Mohammed offers the most accessible example of this process, similar transformations were certainly underway simultaneously among all the diverse Turkish, Mongol, and Tungusic peoples of the northern steppe.

Whenever peaceable relations between grasslands and cropland broke down, raid replaced trade quite automatically. The alternative was imminent starvation for herdsmen who had become dependent on cereal food to expand their caloric intake far above the levels they could derive from their flocks and herds directly. The resulting waves of nomad invasion and conquest that played so large a role in the political history of Eurasia between 300 and 1300 A.D. therefore brought commercially experienced rulers to power. This was true even on the fringes of the civilized world where Viking raiders and Japanese pirates replaced nomad herdsmen as rivals to constituted public authority. But seafaring robbers depended on trade as intimately as nomads had come to do. Only through organized, peaceable exchanges could haphazard hauls of booty be converted into the array of commodities required to outfit ships and crews on an on-going basis, season after season.

Hence the political upheavals so characteristic of the so-called Dark Ages had the effect of making the rulers of the civilized portions of Eurasia far more familiar with, and attuned to, the values of the merchant class than had been true earlier. The spread of Islam is the most conspicuous instance of this change; the conquests of Genghis Khan had a comparable importance further east and north. But even before the Mongol empire gave political expression to the new interconnectedness of steppe and cultivated lands, the kneading of market-regulated behavior into the political command structures of Eurasia achieved a critical breakthrough about the year 1000 A.D. From that time onwards, trade and market exchanges began to enlarge their scope generation after generation in what proved to be a decisive fashion.

The key change probably began in China. Under the Sung dynasty (960-1279 A.D.), the Celestial empire developed a closely articulated exchange economy. China's shift from a command to a market-directed economy was, of course, gradual. The arrival of Buddhist monks, and of traders from Central Asia associated with Buddhism, constituted one critical input, beginning as early as the third century A.D. Another factor was the official decision in 780 to allow conversion of tax income from kind to money payments. Probably most basic of all was the artificial improvement of internal water transport, making movement of goods within China relatively cheap. The great landmark of this process was the completion in 611 of the Grand Canal, connecting the Yangtse and the Yellow rivers. But many lesser engineering works were also necessary before a widely ramified internal communications system up and down the two great rivers of China came securely into existence.

The tax shift from collections in kind to money payments both registered and confirmed the change that came to China's economy. Although this conversion had begun on a small scale and by way of exception in the eighth century, it became predominant soon after 1000 A.D. As the shift to money taxes occurred, officials began to expend tax monies by entering the market and buying goods and services that the government found needful. They thereby returned cash to the private sector, lending the weight of their authority to the further diffusion of market behavior within Chinese society.

Thereupon, all the advantages of specialization that Adam Smith was later to analyze so persuasively began to exercise their dominion across the varied landscapes of the Chinese empire. As efficiency of production grew, so did wealth. The officials of the empire, in effect, discovered (rather to their surprise) that by refraining from interfering with market behavior the government could actually increase its effective command over goods and services. As long as the enhanced wealth created by the commercial integration of China's various regions was still new, and growth continued spontaneously, the political authorities were usually content to let well enough alone. They only intervened occasionally to check private accumulation of capital when flagrant price gouging or some other infraction of Confucian propriety seemed to call for such action. Indirect regulation of price levels by issuance of paper currency was part of Sung official policy, and officials specializing in fiscal management developed a rather sophisticated doctrine about the relation between prices, money, and metallic backing for the paper currency.

If all this seems strikingly modern, I can only say that it was. Indeed I propose to date the onset of modern times from the eleventh century, when this transformation of the Chinese economy and society got firmly under way.

Its effects were not, of course, confined to the provinces that reverently obeyed the Celestial emperor's commands. Neighboring peoples also joined the trade network, coming in as tributaries and subordinates, at least according to Chinese court rituals. Caravan contacts with central and western Asia, the steppes, and India multiplied. Far more significant was the development of seaborne commerce. Ships, as seaworthy as any known to Europeans, sailed to Korea and Japan; others coasted southward to Indonesia, and by the close of the eleventh century direct voyaging to the Indian Ocean from the South China Sea became common.

The effect within this vast sea room was much the same as the effect of improved internal water communications had been within China proper: trade exchanges multiplied, technology diffused, and various kinds of regional specialization expanded total wealth production in coastal regions of eastern and southeastern Asia very substantially. The most important example of this process was the importation of early ripening rice into China proper from the south (by 1012). This permitted rice to grow on hillsides where the spring runoff only lasted a few weeks, thereby enormously increasing the food production of southern China. In well-watered lowlands, early ripening rice allowed double cropping, with equally spectacular results. This massive growth of agricultural productivity meant that tax and rent income from the peasantry expanded (especially in central and south China) *pari passu* with the intensification of mercantile and artisan activity. The older, fundamentally rural, articulation of Chinese society that was centered upon obedience to commands coming from social superiors therefore remained alive and well, and the new commercial and industrial populations never really challenged the primacy of China's traditional ruling class.

Official capacity to intervene in the market remained unquestioned; and when, under the Mongols (who conquered China between 1211 and 1279), economically more reckless managers came to power, a runaway inflation upset the Sung pattern of indirect governmental manipulation of market prices. Paper money was thereby discredited in China for centuries. China's initial development towards large-scale technology and capitalistic organization of trade and industry also suffered crippling shocks, largely through official purchases of strategically important commodities at uneconomic prices. This began before the end of the Sung dynasty, and eventually brought economic growth almost to a halt. Large-scale private wealth survived only when associated with such officially approved enterprises as tax farming—for example, management of the manufacture and distribution of salt. Official actions thus stabilized China's massive surge towards a market economy by about 1500, just when western Europeans, reacting more slowly to intensifying trade exchanges, entered upon their modern, globe-girdling military and commercial adventures.

I must admit that the spectacular economic boom of Sung China did not have any obvious impact on the Middle East. In that ancient center of trade and commerce, Islam had already (from 632) encouraged and sustained a substantial commercial development; and it is probable that the warmer climate of the eleventh through the thirteenth centuries, which improved western European harvests and promoted that region's economic growth, brought damaging drought to Middle Eastern grain fields. At any rate, no sign of an economic boom of the kind that came to the Far East can be discerned in the Islamic heartland; and from the thirteenth century, if not before, Iraq began to suffer economic decline as irrigation canals went out of service.

One might perhaps view what happened in China between 1000 and 1500 as an application to the Far East of patterns of political and commercial symbiosis that were already age-old in the Middle East. The same was far more obviously true of western Europe.

Within the Mediterranean, a new vigor and efficiency of trade developed in the eleventh century when Italian ships took over the task of transporting goods from port to port. Simultaneously, Italians also took over Moslem (and Byzantine) legal regulation of business and details of commercial practices almost without modification. For several centuries, however, European commercial networks remained far less highly developed than those of China. Marco Polo's report of his travels (1271-1295) emphasized the massive scale of Chinese cities. His wonder at the size of everything in that country is evidence of how far the Chinese of the thirteenth century had outstripped the rest of the Eurasian ecumene.

Yet Europe eventually caught up. From the very modest levels of the eleventh century, trade conducted by Latin Christians tended to expand, despite cyclical ups and downs and despite the active distrust of market behavior and the ringing denunciations of usury that churchmen regularly voiced. As Chinese sea commerce began to unite Japan, Korea, and Southeast Asia into a single market area, so, too, the advance of navigation (and some critical political acts) in Europe led to the merging of Mediterranean commerce with the commerce of the Black Sea to the east and of the Atlantic and Baltic to the west. The key date for the opening of the Black Sea was 1204, when

Venetians and a motley company of crusaders captured Constantinople and opened the straits to their ships for the first time. The equivalent date for the opening of the Atlantic waters to Italian enterprise was 1290, when a Genoese buccaneer and businessman, Benedetto Zaccaria, defeated the Moslem authorities who had previously sealed the straits of Gibraltar to Christian shipping. Thereafter the wool trade of northwestern Europe could link up with the spice trade coming into the Mediterranean from the southeast, creating a growingly complex interdependence across very long sea distances and among numerous and diverse political structures.

Even though European commerce remained weaker and less massive than the exchanges sustaining the interregional integration that occurred under the roof of the Chinese imperial state, the fact that Far Western trade patterns ran across innumerable political boundaries gave market-oriented human behavior in Europe a decisive advantage compared to anything enjoyed by Chinese merchants and the producers who fed goods into the private trade nets of China. As we shall presently note in more detail, this was demonstrated in interesting and fateful fashion in the fifteenth century, when Chinese imperial authorities prohibited sea voyaging on the ground that it diverted valuable resources from the more urgent tasks of land defense against a threatening nomad power across the northwest frontier.

Perhaps it may be useful to distinguish two waves in the ecumenical upsurge of market-oriented behavior. One wave rested mainly on overland trade networks reaching from China to eastern Europe by northerly routes across the grassy steppes, as well as by the older oasis-hopping route of the classical Silk Road. This trade net sustained and was sustained by the Mongol empire that briefly brought China, Russia, and lands in between under one political roof. Italian commerce responded by developing Black Sea ports as a major exchange point with the caravan world to the east.

However, this linkage across Eurasia carried its special nemesis in the form of lethal outbreaks of bubonic plague. The arrival of the Black Death in Europe in 1347 is well known, and recent studies show that it took more than 130 years before European populations regained the levels they had attained before the new disease struck. The effect upon steppe populations was far more damaging because their grassy homeland became a permanent reservoir for the plague bacillus—or so I have argued in my book *Plagues and Peoples*[1] to which I should refer you for a fuller discussion of the evidence.

As had happened in the late classical age, when unfamiliar diseases wreaked havoc with population and wealth in the Roman and Chinese worlds, the political register of the die-offs resulting from bubonic exposure among nomads was the disruption of large state structures. The Mongol empire broke up into warring fragments, and the trade net across the steppes was never restored. Central Asia sank towards marginality, economically, politically, and culturally. This was because, in addition to the direct impoverishment due to population losses from disease, a new, second wave of commercial development propagated itself across the seaways with such vigor as to make resumption of overland transport uneconomic, even if local conditions had allowed the caravans to travel once again as freely as they had in Marco Polo's age.

Official Chinese expeditions into the Indian Ocean began on a truly imperial scale early in the fifteenth century, only to be withdrawn and permanently abandoned after 1430 as a result of orders from the imperial court in Peking. The enterprise of Chinese merchants operating from the southern coast could not prevail against official command. Resources, such as gunmetal, needed to equip oceangoing ships, were desired by the imperial majesty for its own uses far to the north; ship building was accordingly abandoned. China's chance to forestall the Portuguese in the Indian Ocean and Columbus in the Americas was thereby foreclosed, simply because the commercial classes of China remained so thoroughly subject to an imperial bureaucracy as to inhibit large-scale independent enterprise on their part.

In the Far West a different development occurred, as is well known. Portuguese ventures down the coast of Africa eventuated in the rounding of the Cape of Good Hope and the discovery of a sea route to India in 1499. Earlier in the decade, by seeking Cathay, Columbus found America and opened a new world to European enterprise. The familiar Commercial Revolution of the sixteenth century ensued, linking American production of gold and silver with European commerce and European commerce with the spices and other precious products of the Indian Ocean. Eventually Japan and the south China coast also entered into the European-managed exchange pattern. Shift of the most active centers of European trade and manufacture from the Mediterranean to northwestern Europe soon followed—a shift completed only in the seventeenth century, with the rise of the English, Dutch, and French trade empires. As a result, the modern integration of the globe into a single market-regulated economy was already well under way by 1700.

Thus China's abdication was Europe's gain. Put another way, the demonstration of the power of the Chinese imperial command system to confine and redirect market-oriented behavior prevented China from taking an active part in the development of a global sea-trade network. Instead, Europeans took over; and their continued exploitation of the wealth-generating possibilities of such trade was sustained by the fact that no single political authority existed in Europe to redirect activity, as had happened in China.

By dominating long-distance sea trade, European merchants concentrated much new wealth in European cities. On top of this, the new regime of the seas provoked a growing primacy of the Far West over other civilizations of the earth on three distinct levels: ideational, microparasitic, and macroparasitic.

First of all, in intellectual matters, Europeans could afford to be curious about the newly apparent diversity of the earth. Since they controlled communications with alien peoples, they felt no immediate threat from the new contacts their seamanship opened up. Instead, any useful novelty that came to their attention could be considered, wondered at, and, if it seemed worthwhile, appropriated for their own use. A systematic openness to new thoughts resulted, whereas in other civilized regions of the earth, when the alien presence seemed menacing to any aspect of inherited values—as happened sooner or later in each case of cultural encounter—a defensive mentality asserted itself that sought to close out everything unfamiliar and dangerous to established verities. Such stubborn conservatism could not compete with the self-confident curiosity that sustained the rapid development of European skills and knowledge until they clearly outstripped all rivals—a situation generally achieved by the eighteenth century.

The circulation of ideas, in other words, took on a new pattern and velocity that was of special advantage to Europeans as a result of the growth of global trade networks. Precisely the same was true of the circulation of microparasites. Disease-experienced regions of the earth, where civilized densities of population and communications networks had already established high levels of immunity to a large number of microparasitic infections, suffered relatively little from the new seaborne contacts. To be sure, ports like London and Lisbon became notorious for their unhealthiness, and indeed periodic epidemics wreaked very great damage to city populations in Europe (and presumably elsewhere) between the fifteenth and eighteenth centuries. But as the frequency of such visitations increased, losses concentrated on younger and younger age groups. Within a couple of centuries, most lethal epidemic diseases became endemic, at least in the largest port centers, so that only infants and small children were likely to die of them. As upcountry trade linkages intensified, larger and larger hinterlands also became increasingly disease-experienced and less liable to suffer disastrous die-off of adult populations when some infection not encountered for a generation or more spread out from an urban bridgehead.

Hence, as infections became more and more homogenized throughout the civilized world, their demographic impact altered in such a way as to facilitate population growth. Children were relatively easy to replace; even high infant mortality rates could be counterbalanced by correspondingly high birth rates. On this basis, civilized populations began to grow whenever and wherever enhanced food production made such growth feasible. This trend became unmistakable sometime during the eighteenth century in both China and Europe; Indian populations probably followed the same curve, but it is unlikely that Middle Eastern communities did so. Perhaps this was because enlargement of food supplies in the Middle East was not as easily achieved as elsewhere, since none of the American food crops—maize, potatoes, sweet potatoes, and the rest—were well suited to the semiarid landscapes that predominate in the Middle East.

In previously isolated parts of the earth, however, the new microparasitic regime inaugurated by oceanic voyaging proved disastrous. Heavy die-off regularly resulted from contact with European and other civilized populations. In many parts of the

earth—North America, Australia, southern Africa, Siberia—
the effect was to empty or nearly empty fertile lands that thus
became available for European settlement. Colonies of settlement—starting for the most part in the seventeenth century—
enormously enhanced the expanse of ground available for European exploitation and reinforced European prosperity by
supplying agricultural goods and raw materials on a rapidly expanding scale in exchange for manufactures issuing from European workshops.

These microparasitic and demographic responses to the new
regime of the seas were matched by similarly drastic changes in
macroparasitic patterns. First of all, the advantages that cavalrymen had enjoyed ever since the ninth century B.C. were
largely nullified by the spread of gunpowder weapons. Steppe
raiding became ineffectual against soldiers armed with guns—
a fact that sealed the shift away from the steppe and towards
the seacoasts as the critical frontier for all parts of the Eurasian
civilized world.

It took a while for this transformation to become irreversi-
ble: it was not until the first half of the seventeenth century that
the eclipse of steppe cavalry tactics became an accomplished
fact. The Chinese and Russian empires were the two states that
gained most from this shift of fortunes between agricultural
and nomad war-making capacity. Accordingly, during the
course of the seventeenth and eighteenth centuries, they expanded their landward frontiers across the interior of Asia until
they fetched up against one another and inaugurated a series of
clashes that have not yet reached definitive resolution.

More important in the short run was the diffusion of cannon,
which occurred with the earliest arrival of European ships on
the coasts of Asia. Here was a weapon that allowed its posses-
sor to knock holes in castle walls within a few hours of its successful emplacement. By monopolizing control of big guns, a

monarch could assure himself of hitherto unattainable superiority over local rivals. In case of quarrel, the *ultimo ratio regis* could come into play—after only a few months of delay—anywhere that existing means of transport would allow big guns to go.

The practical effect was the establishment of a series of what can properly be termed gunpowder empires, whose size and stability against rebellion from within was far greater than anything before possible. The consolidation of Japan under Hideyoshi (d. 1596) and the Tokugawa shoguns is the clearest example of how decisive gunpowder weapons could be in forwarding political consolidation. But the Ming empire in China (1369-1644) and its successor the Ching (1644-1912), no less than the Mughal empire of India (1526-1857) and the Ottoman empire of the eastern Mediterranean and adjacent parts of the Middle East (1453-1923) were other notable examples of the species. And so, for that matter, was Muscovy (1480-1917); while the Portuguese and Spanish overseas empires differed only in depending on cannon-carrying ships to unite the provinces with the capital.

In western Europe, however, the thrust towards the creation of a single political authority misfired. Despite his impressive dominions in Europe and the Americas, Emperor Charles V (1519-1556) failed to consolidate his power over Germany, much less to conquer France; his son, Philip II of Spain (1556-1598), could not even keep the Dutch under his control. Thus western Europe's political diversity survived the gunpowder revolution as happened nowhere else in the civilized world.

Why this should have been so is a matter deserving more careful consideration than I can give here. Technical factors certainly mattered. For example, Europe's precocious development of hard rock mining (compared to that of other civilizations), dating back at least to the eleventh century, meant that many different sources of gunmetal existed, so that no one ruler could easily monopolize access to the copper, tin, and zinc needed for casting big guns. More decisive still was the fact that in the first decades of the sixteenth century, ingenious Italian architects discovered that revetments of earth could protect stone walls from the destructive force of gunfire. By combining this with crossfire from heavily gunned bastions and a dry ditch to defend against escalade, the advantage to the attacker that cannon had briefly conferred was abruptly cancelled. As a result, after the 1520s, long and difficult sieges again became normal in European warfare wherever local authorities could afford the new style of fortification. Possession of a few big guns no longer sufficed to assure superiority over local defenses of any and every kind, as remained the case in other parts of the world.

Europe's continued political fragmentation meant that wars and preparations for wars continued to bulk very large in the public life of that part of the civilized world. A steady thrust after improvements in armament and military technique was one result. An elaborate and rapidly evolving art of war soon allowed European states to outstrip the gunpowder empires of Asia, where internal stimulus to improvement of armament design and military organization disappeared as soon as a single imperial center had effectually monopolized existing stocks of heavy artillery. As a result, by the eighteenth century or earlier, European land forces had attained a clear superiority over all rivals, matching the military superiority their ships had enjoyed from the time they first approached the shores of Asia.

There was still another aspect to Europe's political pluralism. No single sovereign could do much to subordinate mercantile and commercial activity to his own purposes. Taxation, if too heavy in one place, speedily led to flight of capital and trade to another location where costs of doing business were less.

Hence, before the twentieth century, the autonomy of market-oriented activity vis-à-vis political command structures never came seriously into question.

The result was to maintain a far greater scope for market-regulated behavior in western Europe than was common in other parts of the civilized world. This in turn gave freer rein to the efficiency that private initiative and self-interest brought to the tasks of assorting and manufacturing goods and distributing services. Yet the rapid growth in the range and massiveness of market-regulated behavior did not prevent European command structures from also enhancing their power by creating more and more effective armies and navies. There is no need to underline the uniqueness of a situation in which the choice between guns and butter did not have to be made. The total wealth of western Europe rapidly increased, and in such a way that increases in taxation lagged far enough behind increases in wealth to allow spectacular expansion of privately owned and managed capital. Sung China had approached this condition too for a while, but private businessmen in China never won as much autonomy from their political superiors, nor accumulated capital on as large a scale, as European entrepreneurs managed to do in early modern times.

I would like to pause for a moment to emphasize how atypical the relationship between rulers and businessmen in western Europe really was. By about 1500, even the mightiest European rulers actually came to depend on traders and bankers for the means of organizing an efficient army. Instead of taxing away available wealth as was the norm in other civilized lands when military need asserted itself, western monarchs found themselves caught in the toils of private wheelers and dealers who insisted on making a profit on every transaction—or at least of seeing a good chance of making a profit. Rulers were actually unable to exert their sovereign power in war without soliciting loans from private persons who were usually domiciled beyond the bounds of the ruler's own jurisdiction and thus safe from confiscatory taxation. As early as the eleventh century in several important European cities, merchants became local sovereigns. Such city states offered initial havens for capital accumulation. Then, at a later time, in larger states like Holland and England, men whose wealth depended on buying and selling in the marketplace proved capable of defending themselves in war against indubitably legitimate political sovereigns who tried to assess new and burdensome taxes. This was, after all, a central issue in both the Dutch revolt of the sixteenth century and the English civil war of the seventeenth.

Many factors contributed to the autonomy that market-regulated behavior continued to enjoy in western Europe, and I do not mean to reduce everything to the survival of political pluralism. Still, it does seem to me that the European state system was crucial in preventing the takeover of mercantile wealth by bureaucratic authority in the way Chinese, Mughal, and Ottoman officials were able to do as a matter of course. In these imperial states, and in Spain as well, trade crossing jurisdictional borders fell into the hands of foreigners whose base of operation lay safely beyond reach of confiscatory taxation. Within the state itself, trade and manufacture was forced back toward retail and handicraft levels because any conspicuous concentration of capital (in anything other than land) swiftly attracted the tax collector's attention, making large-scale transactions on a private basis (except for tax farming) well nigh impossible. Whenever government authorities wanted to concentrate resources—characteristically to equip and maintain an army—resort to compulsory corvée and levies in kind were necessary. Goods coming freely to market could not do more than sustain a retail supply of food and other necessary materials for city populations—and that, often, precariously.

By contrast, the growing power of European market-regulated behavior meant that larger and larger enterprises could be mounted by assembling goods and manpower in response to perceived private advantage. There was not, however, any simple dichotomy between public and private, bureaucratic and capitalistic management. On the contrary, private pursuit of profit and public administration could be and were merged by such bodies as the Dutch and English East India Companies, each of which came to exercise sovereign authority overseas. Indeed, as the scale of their operations increased, economic organizations aimed at private profit normally took on bureaucratic features that made them imperfectly distinguishable from governmental command systems. From the governmental side, European public officials often found it best to rely on market inducements when they sought to assemble the goods and services the sovereign authority required for its own purposes. Accordingly, corvée and other political ways of overriding spontaneous response to market incentives shrank in importance, though in practice compulsion was never entirely eschewed, especially when it came to recruitment into armies and navies.

The general effect, it seems obvious, was to improve the efficiency with which goods and services could be marshalled for large-scale undertakings. Amazingly, state power increased as compulsion diminished! Wealth increased as more massive and more mobile capital allowed new technologies, economies of scale, and interregional specialization to reinforce one another. In short, between the fourteenth and twentieth centuries, acceleration of Europe's capacity to produce wealth became autocatalytic—a self-sustaining process, perhaps best compared to the reaction of an atomic pile when one considers the disruptive consequences Europe's increasing wealth and power had for the rest of the world.

Within Europe itself, those states that gave the most scope

to private capital and entrepreneurship prospered the most, whereas better governed societies in which welfare on the one hand or warfare on the other commanded a larger proportion of available resources tended to lag behind. After 1600, for example, Italian cities like Venice, where state policy protected the poor from the worst hardships of their condition, and militarized empires like those of Spain, Muscovy, and the Hapsburg cluster in central Europe all failed to keep pace with the economic development of such conspicuously undergoverned lands as Holland and England.

Diversification between a growingly powerful center and economically subordinated peripheral regions became a self-confirming, self-reinforcing pattern. Goods and services exchanged between center and periphery sustained continued growth of private capital at the center. This was so because toward the periphery the needs of the state were more clamant, taxation and bureaucratic regulation were more constricting, and skill remained in short supply. These differentials were also maintained by migration of entrepreneurs and of capital towards those central locations where conditions for making a fortune were most propitious. Sometimes, of course, private pursuit of wealth meant directing resources to distant places to start up mines or other new enterprises; more often it pulled entrepreneurs and capital towards a few urban centers in northwestern Europe where market exchanges were already most intense and where private wealth was already most secure against forcible expropriation.

All of these complex circumstances conducing to the expansion of European wealth and power were reinforced after the middle of the eighteenth century by what we are accustomed to refer to as the Industrial Revolution. Machinery using first water and then steam power cheapened goods enormously, allowing an increase of their quantity far beyond earlier possibilities. How drastic the result could be is well illustrated by a remark Robert Owen made in his *Autobiography* to the effect that cotton cloth costing half a guinea a yard in the 1790s could be purchased for two pence a yard in the 1850s—that is, for 1/63 of its earlier price. This makes it obvious why English manufacturers were able to undersell highly skilled Indian weavers on their own home ground by the early nineteenth century.

European merchants thus acquired a new weapon to upset existing social structures in other parts of the world in the form of a vast supply of goods that were far cheaper (and sometimes better) than anything that could be produced locally. Asian and African artisans suffered more directly. But change went far beyond the destruction of their prosperity: the sudden availability of new and cheaper goods, enlarged transportation capacities, and pressures to organize the production of raw materials and other goods that European merchants wanted to take in exchange for their proffered manufactures set the societies of all the rest of the earth into motion, often in ways that local rulers and old elites found distressing.

Yet efforts to check European economic penetration were seldom successful for long. Even in the eighteenth century, European states were ready and able to send armed forces to distant parts of the earth to support the interests of their merchants. In the nineteenth century, the technical equipment and disciplined art of war at the disposal of European expeditionary forces became overwhelmingly superior to arms and military organization available elsewhere. This became fully manifest in the 1840s when the British easily defeated Chinese defenders of Canton. The costs of such an action actually became trivial from the point of view of European state treasuries, committed, as they had been since the seventeenth century, to the maintenance of standing armies and navies. Hence the notorious "absence of mind" with which European empires expanded in the second half of the nineteenth century, until nearly all the globe had submitted to political as well as economic management from west European centers.

European imperialism was enormously facilitated by the fact that Europe's new surge of power arising from the Industrial Revolution coincided in time with what may be described as a "natural" rhythm of imperial decay in Asia. Gunpowder empires that had sprung into existence in the sixteenth and seventeenth centuries in the wake of the initial diffusion of cannon around the earth were all suffering from serious internal ailments by the late eighteenth century. Except in Japan, these empires had been founded by small warrior elites whose language and culture were alien to the great majority of their subjects. With time, the cohesion and military efficiency of such ruling groups diminished—the sweets of civilization being preferable to the hardships of military discipline. Governmental weakness and insecurity naturally resulted in both India and China. Another disturbing factor was the massive increase in peasant numbers, largely due to homogenization of infections. The result was to bring on a general crisis of Asian regimes so that by 1850 or so even the mightiest of them could offer only token resistance to European intrusion. Thus the extraordinary European world hegemony of the years 1850 to 1914 was partly illusory—a result of an accidental coincidence of Europe's new wealth and power with a period of exceptional weakness among Asian governments and ruling elites.

I should add, perhaps, that even though European rulers and state officials in the nineteenth century did not begin to sop up all of the new forms of wealth that burgeoned so luxuriantly in the lee of the Industrial Revolution, allowing private capital and levels of consumption to grow to unprecedented heights, still it was also true that new ideas and principles of political management expanded the range of public power over private citizens very greatly. For example, before the French Revolution, ordinary subjects had been immune from military service. From the upper classes, only volunteers entered armies and navies; conscription, which was needed to fill the lower ranks, was confined to specially disadvantaged classes of the population, such as the urban unemployed, landless peasants, merchant-seamen, and the like.

The French Revolution changed all that, making liability to military conscription the price of citizenship—at least for young males. Liberal revolution also swept away a multitude of privileged corporations and statuses that had previously limited the jurisdiction of state officials. By making everyone equal in law, everyone became equally free, and also equally liable to compulsory state service. For a few decades, the freedom arising from removal of older social barriers and differentiations was more apparent than the new subordination to centralized direction that liberal and democratic principles of government also implied. The potential for a political capture of the enhanced human and material resources the Industrial Revolution made available became apparent only in the twentieth century. This is, in turn, part of a larger readjustment whereby the recent decades of world history have begun to redress the exceptional lopsidedness of global relationships that worked so remarkably in Europe's favor between 1500 and 1900.

Taking the microparasitic side of things first, the central event of our time was the dramatic reduction of infant mortality, first in the Western world, then throughout most of the globe. This was due to the application of public health measures, beginning about 1850 but attaining a truly global scale only in our own time, mainly since 1945. Once medical researchers were able to decipher patterns of infection—the first human disease to be so deciphered was cholera, in 1884—

cheap and effective ways of interrupting the chain of infection were soon devised: vaccination, pasteurization, hand washing, and the like. The childhood diseases of civilization ceased to matter very much when confronted by such countermeasures. Infants ceased to die in the old-fashioned way, with consequences well-known to worried demographers and ecologists. The resultant population explosions in Asia, Africa, and Latin America are fundamental disturbers of world balances today, and will remain so for some time to come.

Yet countervailing forces are not absent. Microorganisms have a way of speedily circumventing medical and chemical attack, since their short life cycles allow rapid genetic change when some radically new selective pressure is brought to bear upon them. The recrudescence of malaria in regions where it was once thought to have been banished is perhaps the most important example of this tendency for natural balances to reassert themselves even in face of modern scientific techniques. Other kinds of disease, too, have arisen to replace the one-time formidable infectious diseases of childhood, although most of these manifest themselves mainly among adults—cancer, for example. Disease, in short, remains a significant factor in human ecology, despite the radical shifts in its incidence that the propagation of scientific medicine provoked during the last hundred years.

On the macroparasitic side, too, the extraordinary domination that market-regulated behavior enjoyed in Europe between the fourteenth and nineteenth centuries has clearly begun to meet with enhanced resistances. These arise partly from within the dominating societies, and on two levels. Most striking of these, perhaps, is the way in which corporations pursuing profit have themselves evolved from small-scale individual- or family-managed companies into bureaucratic command structures. Large business corporations do not respond internally to market direction in any very obvious way, even though managers are accustomed to measure their success in terms of a balance sheet derived from the "foreign" transactions such corporations may have made with other similar corporations as well as with governments and small-scale retailers. Managed prices set for transactions that occur within such corporations can often be extended to transactions with outsiders. This is especially true when the purchaser is a government (also bureaucratically organized) and when the goods or services offered for sale are such that only a few suppliers (or perhaps even a single supplier) can provide them.

This internal dynamic of capitalist organization was matched by the way in which converging considerations of warfare and welfare have led to pervasive public intervention in market processes. Here the great landmark was World War I (1914-1918), when men and things were mobilized on a scale and with a rigor undreamed of earlier. During this period, war and social welfare came to be closely linked: when munitions factories mattered as much as army divisions for winning the war, administrative measures designed to promote troop welfare could logically be expanded to apply to civilians as well. This was normalized during World War II (1939-1945), when all the major belligerents resorted to rationing and, almost inadvertently, thereby equalized access to many scarce commodities for rich and poor alike. War experience of state socialism was carried over into peacetime (especially during the economic depression of the 1930s) with varying degrees of rigor, depending on how effectively the prevailing political system mobilized lower-class aspirations for greater economic equality.

Resistance to the regime of the market also mounted in the peripheral regions of the earth where weakness and poverty of the past was widely resented by those peoples who had been compelled to submit to political or economic dependence. The critical landmark here, too, dates back to World War I, when Russian revolutionaries set out to repudiate the tyranny of the market in the name of justice, equality, and a more perfect freedom. In practice, Russian Communism owed more to patterns of war mobilization than to Marxist ideals, for Lenin and his heirs carried forward into peacetime and normalized the bureaucratic patterns of state socialism and manpower mobilization that had been invented in World War I.

It looks, therefore, as though our own age has witnessed a rapid readjustment of balance between market-directed and bureaucratically directed behavior that comes closer to what may properly be regarded as the civilizational norm—assuming that the behavior of most civilized states and peoples most of the time is the appropriate definition of the norm. If so, a probable consequence will be a fairly rapid slowdown of technical and other changes, for bureaucracies characteristically resist disturbances of routine and are powerful enough to make their distaste for innovation effective. Competition among rival states and among rival corporations is what now inhibits bureaucratic conservatism. Such competition may of course continue to push rival command systems to seek some advantage by everrenewed efforts at technical and organizational change, but agreements to limit such efforts are likewise conceivable—either tacit or formalized into treaties (like SALT I and II) and cartels.

Indeed, it is easy to imagine a time not far in the future when existing public and private bureaucracies might come together into a self-perpetuating structure aimed first and foremost at keeping things as nearly stable as possible by guarding the privileges and power of existing managerial elites around the globe. If this should happen, market-regulated behavior will swiftly be cribbed, cabined, and confined to the interstices of society. This is exactly where it belonged in civilized state systems before

1000 A.D., when the modern expansion and eventual runaway explosion (seventeenth to nineteenth centuries) of market behavior began.

Such a vision of the past and future does not really suggest, however, that stability across long centuries lies ahead. Too many violent upheavals of ecological patterns have been set in motion by humanity's recent breakaway from older modes of life for even a very skilled managerial bureaucracy to navigate the future without confronting—perhaps often exacerbating—large-scale crises. Accessibility of cheap birth control devices means that recent population growth is quite likely to yield to population collapse, if young women reacting against their mothers' enslavement to the cradle cease to find the heavy task of nurturing infants worth their while. A pattern whereby in some parts of the world human reproduction falls below replacement levels while existing growth patterns persist elsewhere is even more probable for the near future—that is, across the next fifty to one hundred years. Such conditions will obviously set the scene for *Völkerwanderungen* of a massive kind, whether in the wake of wars or through individual and family migrations.

Raw material shortages are no less likely to harass our descendants in ways more severe than anything we have yet glimpsed in the form of petroleum supply difficulties. The industrial era of the past two hundred years may in retrospect appear to be the work of spendthrift generations who mined fuels and minerals recklessly and with consequences for natural balances that only millennia will be able to heal.

Humanity, in short, is not likely to run out of problems to confront nor of changes needing to be made in prevailing practices, even if market behavior—the main motor of recent social and economic change—should disengage from the driveshaft of global society. Action and reaction within a complex ecological web will not cease, and efforts to understand its functioning fully and to foresee future side effects will continue to elude human capacity for some time to come, and perhaps forever.

As long as these circumstances persist, stability will remain unattainable in human affairs, however much rulers and managers may desire it. Like all other forms of life, humankind remains inextricably entangled in flows of matter and energy that result from eating and being eaten. However clever we have been in finding new niches in that system, the enveloping microparasitic-macroparasitic balances limiting human access to food and energy have not been abolished, and never will be.

. . .

To emphasize that fact and to improve our understanding of humanity's revolutionary record within the web of life that spreads so precariously and magnificently over the earth's surface has been the goal and purpose of these lectures. If the vision of the human condition I impart seems gloomy, deterministic, and unattractive, I regret it. Personally I feel quite the opposite, finding a certain enlargement of the spirit in recognizing my own and all humanity's kinship with other forms of life, while also admiring the manner in which social interactions, symbolic meanings, and human intelligence have allowed an otherwise unimpressive species to transform the conditions of life over and over again—for ourselves, and for nearly all the other animals and plants that share the earth with us.

Surely the remarkable power of mind, of culture, and of the meaningful word to alter material processes is dramatically demonstrated by humanity's historic role in altering the face of the earth. In weaving these words together to make this presentation I, too, attest my lively faith in the power of words to alter the way human beings think and act. What we believe about the past, after all, does much to define how we behave in the present and what we do towards making up the future. If these lectures contribute even in a small way to improving the adequacy of our hindsight, I will be well pleased. Better hindsight deepens insight and makes for a less imperfect foresight. It thus improves the human condition, and to this, surely, we all aspire.

PART III

Control and Catastrophe in Human Affairs

CATASTROPHE OBVIOUSLY plays a big role in human affairs, manifesting itself in social relations, profoundly affecting both economics and politics. The historical record, indeed, seems to amount to little else than one catastrophe after another, if we mean by catastrophe some sequence of events that disrupts established routines of life and inflicts suffering or death on many.

Ever since civilization arose, leaving decipherable records that allow us to understand something of what people have experienced, catastrophes have been chronic and all but continual. Famine, epidemic, and/or war have affected nearly every participant in civilized society at some time. Despite all the skills we now command, a life immune from exposure to one or more of these catastrophes remains unusual. Perhaps we should recognize that risk of catastrophe is the underside of the human condition—a price we pay for being able to alter natural balances and to transform the face of the earth through collective effort and the use of tools.

A simple example from water engineering may make this situation obvious. In my lifetime the Army Corps of Engineers began to control Mississippi floods by building an elaborate system of levees along the river's lower course. This had the undesired effect of concentrating sediment on the river bottom between the levees. As a result, the water level now rises each year, and the levees have to be raised higher from time to time. Under this regimen, sooner or later the mighty Mississippi will break its banks and inflict far greater damage on the surrounding landscape than if there were no levees and the river were free to overflow each spring and deposit sediment across the breadth of its natural floodplain, as it did in my childhood. Chinese engineers, who began to confine the Yellow River between levees as long ago as 600 B.C., have witnessed this sort of catastrophe several times in recorded history. The superior earth-moving resources of modern technology do not seem at all likely to be able to compensate—indefinitely—for the increasing instability of a river being artificially lifted higher and higher above the adjacent floodplain.

Intelligence and ingenuity in this and innumerable other cases run a race with all the nasty eventualities that interfere with human hopes and purposes; it is far from clear which is winning. Both intelligence and catastrophe appear to move in a world of unlimited permutation and combination, provoking an open-ended sequence of challenge and response. Human history thus becomes an extraordinary, dynamic equilibrium in which triumph and disaster recur perpetually on an ever-increasing scale as our skills and knowledge grow.

This sort of pattern is readily apparent in economics. To begin with, the great human advances were technological. Because they required the concerted effort of thousands of persons, cooperation was achieved by obedience to the commands of a ruler, backed ultimately by the threat of force. Catastrophes had their place in these early command economies, since the armies assembled for war, or for work on some vast construction project, were vulnerable to epidemic disease. Also, crops could always fail and provoke famine. Civilized communities learned to live with such disasters by supporting family systems that encouraged the high birthrates needed to replace these population losses.

For the first 4,000 years of civilized history, private initiatives remained marginal though important. Merchants and other adventurers carried skills, ideas, and goods across political boundaries; sporadic diffusion of civilization resulted. Still, for millennia, producing for distant markets, depending on goods brought from afar, was too risky to sustain ordinary human life. Luxuries and a few critical strategic materials—copper and tin primarily—did in fact travel long distances, but that was all.

Beginning about 1000 A.D. improved transportation changed the situation fundamentally. Articles of common consumption began to enter trade networks—wool, cotton, salt, timber, fish, grain, and the like—on unprecedented scale, and large numbers of people became dependent on food and other commodities brought from afar. Thus the market first supplemented and then supplanted the age-old pattern of obedience to the command of a leader as the regulator of everyday activity for increasing numbers of ordinary people in the thickly populated parts of Eurasia. With this advance (and it was an enormous advance, creating new wealth by allowing specialized production to achieve all the economies that Adam Smith analyzed so persuasively in *The Wealth of Nations*) came a new form of catastrophe—the occasional paralyzing financial crisis.

Periodic crashes of the credit system on which long-distance trade depended began to show up at least as early as the fourteenth century and have continued into our own time. Economic activity has altered in very diverse ways since the fourteenth century, but an irregular four- to five-year alternation between boom and bust has persisted throughout all such changes. The pattern has upset innumerable lives by benefiting a few and hurting the great majority, whose means of livelihood have temporarily collapsed because of panic.

Economists of the late nineteenth and the twentieth centuries have devoted much effort to figuring out how and why this pattern has continued. Since about 1950, countermeasures have softened the impact of what may now be called old-fashioned credit crises, thanks, in large part, to the theoretical understanding economists have been able to work out. The prestige they enjoy in our society today rests on this achievement, even though defects in their foresight have recently become so conspicuous as to call the adequacy of accepted theories into question.

Questions have arisen because, in addition to the four- to five-year business cycles, other, longer-term changes of behavior create larger and more recalcitrant rhythms of economic expansion and downturn in the market. Recent examples are the crash of 1873 and the hard times that prevailed thereafter until the 1890s, and the decade of depression that followed the 1929 crash.

In each case, hard times were followed by a boom that dimmed the effect of the familiar, short-term crises for a generation or so. In retrospect, one may see why. The surge in wealth during the first three decades of the twentieth century probably occurred because of new forms of management and control invented in the aftermath of the 1873 crash. Alfred Chandler's book *The Visible Hand* explains what happened with magnificent precision and insight. In brief, a few ambitious captains of industry built up large corporations that soon dominated the manufacture and sale of such commodities as steel, chemicals, sewing machines, and automobiles. They took full advantage of economies of scale that the latest machinery permitted, and organized a smooth assembly-line flow of all the factors of production—raw material, fuel, labor, and, when appropriate, parts produced elsewhere. Vertical integration allowed a single manager to decide how much raw material was needed and how much or how many end products to offer for sale. If need be, he could cut back production to maintain prices or expand production and lower prices so as to sell more.

When a few such corporations were able to dominate their markets, economies of scale lowered costs very sharply, and such lowered costs were passed on to consumers, at least in part. Both corporate profits and ordinary living standards rose accordingly, but critical advantages remained in the hands of corporation managers. Big corporations were cushioned against short-term credit crises by their managers' ability to adjust output to sales and to fix the prices at which they chose to sell to outsiders. As long as such outsiders were numerous and unorganized, industrial corporation managers could make their plans and reality match up with unprecedented accuracy. The business cycle was not eliminated, but it became catastrophic only for small producers and for those employees who lost their jobs in bad times. In well-managed corporations, however, technical and financial planning foresaw and guarded against temporary inconveniences arising from the ups and downs of the business cycle.

Thus, as long as most of the population farmed and could revert to a quasi-subsistence mode of life in times of credit collapse, corporate management of large-scale industrial production could avert most of the costs of the business cycle from themselves while improving ordinary citizens' lives by cheapening old products and creating new consumer goods. This achievement transformed industrial society profoundly between the 1880s and the 1930s.

Yet corporate management of production and sales had its limitations. A big corporation selling to a government or to another equally well-managed corporation had trouble fixing its sale prices at will. Managers' power to control results was weakened when a large proportion of total output went to other corporations or to the government, for such purchasers were liable to bargain hard over prices and attach other conditions to delivery and payment. As more and more of the business world achieved corporate organization, such dealings multiplied, and the effective autonomy of individual corporations diminished accordingly. To flourish freely and realize their managers' plans exactly, corporations needed a matrix of unorganized buyers and sellers with whom to do business. But the rapid proliferation of corporate business organization that resulted from spectacular early successes had the effect of thinning that unorganized matrix, whereupon corporate managers began to encounter intractable new problems. The perils of the marketplace thus crept back into corporate boardrooms.

The result was the crash and stubborn depression of the 1930s. Dismissing workers and cutting back production while holding prices steady, or nearly steady, did not work when the agricultural, family, and small-firm segment of the economy ceased being able to sustain the shock of credit crunch. Instead, corporate policies intensified the depression, since dismissing workers diminished purchasing power, and that meant fewer sales, dictating further cutbacks in employment and further reduction of available purchasing power. The prevailing corporate policies for surviving bad times therefore created a vicious circle for which there was no ready cure. In time, even the biggest and best-managed corporations began to feel the pinch. Managers had not counted on or prepared for prolonged depression. Their method of guarding against ordinary credit collapses simply intensified the big crash when it came.

Thus, market catastrophe, bigger and more stubborn than before, was able to threaten even the largest corporations, and for a full decade no one in the United States knew what to do, in spite of numerous New Deal efforts to blunt the human costs of the depression. Only in Germany did a brutal new political regime prove itself capable of curing unemployment, but, as we all know, Nazi economic success in the 1930s swiftly provoked a new and far greater political catastrophe in the 1940s.

Nonetheless, economic management on a nationwide scale was sufficiently perfected during World War II to provide the basis for a swift postwar recovery followed by a boom that lasted into the 1970s. New concepts—the gross national product (GNP), for example—and new statistical measuring rods were created to allow skills that had been developed for the management of big corporations to direct the economic effort of entire nations. During the war, the new managers—government officials, often recruited from private industry to begin with—handled the nation and all available material resources as a single firm had been accustomed to treat the labor and raw materials required for large-scale industrial production and had the additional advantage of controlling money and credit within very broad limits.

The nation-as-firm was not completely sovereign, since economic and strategic planning transcended national boundaries on both Allied and Axis sides. But transnational implementation remained shaky, especially among the Axis powers, and after the war it was the national unit of management that prevailed, using macroeconomic concepts and statistical data introduced initially for war mobilization. The Soviet Union was both precocious and backward. Socialist planning had been introduced as early as 1928, but Soviet economic managers remained more reliant on command and compulsion than Western countries, where control of credit became crucial. In Western Europe, on the other hand, transnational integration revived and was carried further than elsewhere, but the constituent national units of the European Economic Community retained veto power over common policies, and each government continued to exercise credit and other controls independently, though not without extensive mutual consultation.

The nationwide scale of economic managment that emerged from the depression of the 1930s and World War II seems very like the enlarged corporate scale of management that emerged from the crash of 1873 and the depressed decades that followed. And the limits of this new way of minimizing exposure to the perils of the marketplace may well turn out to be similar.

One can see already that the spectacular economic success achieved by the leading Western countries and by Japan after 1950 occurred in the context of a much less well-organized Third World. How important that context was for the increase in living standards and GNP of the leading industrial countries is debatable. But it is hard to doubt that raw material suppliers in the Third World and that immigrant laborers coming from poor and mainly agricultural countries bore a disproportionate share of the costs of the fluctuations in the business cycle that persisted in spite of all the deliberate countermeasures that Keynesian and post-Keynesian economists devised. The well-managed industrial nations, like the large, prosperous corporations of the early twentieth century, were effectually insulated from such disturbances by the policies of their managers. The brunt of such catastrophes passed off onto others.

Whether such parallels will provoke another general economic crisis is unclear. It seems possible, for the world's finances are surely in disarray. Third World debt is largely unrepayable, even if the poor nations were willing to try to pay. The financial difficulties facing countries like Poland, Mexico, and Brazil are more significant, since their debts are much larger. United States indebtedness, both governmental and private, is most critical of all and seems sure to result in the disguised repudiation of inflation.

Probably no one knows just what the effect of wholesale debt repudiation would be on the financial system of the world. But it looks as though the economically well-managed nations of the postwar era were in imminent danger of losing the safety valve they enjoyed as long as they acted within the context of poorer, less well-organized trading partners who accepted the prices and terms of trade offered to them in return for an escalating series of loans—loans that now threaten to become unsupportable. In 1929, private citizens who bought cars and other goods on what were then newfangled installment plans were in much the same situation as the world's poor countries are today. But since debtor nations are not nearly so numerous as persons in debt, the parallel should not be pressed too far.

All I wish to suggest is that twice in the past century a very successful response to one sort of market catastrophe, making simple recurrence of the old sort of breakdown unlikely or impossible, has shifted the burden of malfunction onto less well-organized participants in the economic exchange network, and when the disadvantaged became unable to bear the burden, then market catastrophe engulfed even the better-organized, larger units of management, creating a new and more baffling crisis in the system as a whole.

Should we then accept the conservation of catastrophe as a reality in human affairs? The hypothesis strikes me as worth exploring. As long as a majority of the participants in the market system could fall back on local subsistence from agriculture when credit collapsed, periodic crises were not threatening to the economic system as a whole. When, however, a large number of persons severed connection with rural subsistence agriculture, business cycles became far more life threatening and new forms of organization had to be invented to minimize the danger. Public relief was the first response; the rise of big corporations and more extended management of economic processes, industry by industry, was another. But, now it appears that these new organizational forms of production and distribution may eventually encounter stumbling blocks, triggering new forms of crisis.

One cannot say for sure that the quantity or severity of the resulting market catastrophe was the same as what arose in earlier times when small-scale actors dominated the scene. Fewer breakdowns, lasting longer and being more difficult to recover from, may add up to about the same total of human suffering and dislocation. On the other hand, they may not. Comparing radically different standards of living in different times and places is difficult. Perhaps, therefore, the notion of the conservation of catastrophe ought only to be entertained as a rhetorical reminder of the refractory character of human behavior even when managed with all the rationality and foresight of which we are capable.

.   .   .

REFRACTORINESS to rational management is not limited to economics. The tendency toward conservation of catastrophe seems rather more evident in the political than in the economic field, for the better organized a government is at home and the better it is able to keep the peace domestically, the more capable it is of waging war abroad. Even if periods of peace make outbreaks of violence less frequent, their scale, when they do occur, is certain to increase.

Yet amidst the incessant tumult of political struggles that dominate the historical record, we detect one clear pattern that seems to contradict this observation: the emergence of large empires whose rulers have been content to use minimal armed force for the defense of their far-flung frontiers and have often preferred bribery to force in their dealings with neighboring barbarians. "Universal states" of this sort, to use a term Toynbee invented, arise through war and, in due season, perish through war. But for periods of several centuries, such states have been able to banish organized violence from large areas of the earth and reduce political catastrophe to comparatively trivial proportions.

For heirs of the European tradition, the Roman Empire is the obvious archetype of a universal state; but very exact parallels to the rise of Roman power over the ancient Mediterranean world are to be found in Mesopotamian, Indian, and Chinese antiquity and in the Amerindian history of both Peru and Mexico. The prominence and regularity of this political pattern inspired Toynbee to make it a key to all history—a burden it cannot really bear since there are parts of the world and eras of time in which local warfare and other forms of political struggle have been altered fundamentally by influences coming from somewhere outside the civilization concerned. The rise of Islam is one of the most remarkable examples of such a transforming force, and Spain's New World conquests of the early sixteenth century are another.

Many thoughtful observers of the recent history of the world have wondered whether the pattern of the rise of states to imperial hegemony may not reassert itself, this time on a truly worldwide scale. Ever since about 1500 in Europe, for instance, military and political history can be understood as a series of bids for imperial hegemony. All have failed, sometimes only narrowly, but the propensity remains inherent in the rivalries of the state system itself.

Short of world empire, and the bureaucratic management of both economic and military affairs on a global scale that such an empire would have to inaugurate, it is hard to see how new organizational inventions could resolve contemporary difficulties in a way analogous to that in which larger and larger states on the one hand, and larger and larger units of economic management on the other, have hitherto responded to recurrent catastrophe. But the future is always opaque, and some still unimagined change—catastrophic or not—may entirely alter human affairs—politically, economically, epidemiologically, environmentally, or even psychologically. For I need not remind you that economics and politics do not embrace all dimensions of human activity, even though I have chosen to illustrate the race between intelligence and catastrophe from that limited angle of vision.

. . .

LET ME therefore draw back a bit and try to reflect in very general terms about the power of human beings to alter their lives and environment so as to banish catastrophe and about the limits of that power. It seems clear to me that the more successful a group of human beings is in avoiding catastrophe by using their powers of organization, foresight, and calculation, the greater become the catastrophes they invite by colliding with similarly organized and managed human groups. And if we imagine a world in which the entire human race were somehow organized so as to banish war and avert economic crisis, it seems likely that other kinds of catastrophe—perhaps greater than ever—might arise because of collisions between a newly organized humanity and the rest of the ecosystem of the planet.

Human affairs seem to proceed within a complex hierarchy of equilibria. We are parts of the physical and chemical world, after all; and atoms and molecules maintain a very reliable equilibrium in the neighborhood of our planet, at least for the time being. The law of entropy suggests that these equilibria will not last forever, but on a human and terrestrial time scale we can afford to treat them as stable and given. Far more volatile are the ecological and what I will call the semiotic equilibria within which human lives and societies exist, and it is at this level that public affairs arise and have their being.

The ecological equilibrium results from flows of matter and energy among living things. The food chain, whereby organisms feed on one another, is its central feature. The role of plants in using the energy of sunlight to synthesize organic compounds connects the ecological equilibrium firmly with the chemical and physical levels of organization. The body chemistry of animals is likewise rooted in what I like to think of as the same lower order of organization. The pyramid is then completed by a semiotic equilibrium perched precariously on top of the ecological equilibrium. It is constituted by the flow of symbolic messages that human beings rely on for regulating their everyday activity and collective behavior.

The interaction among these different levels of organization is very little understood. The recent advances in biochemistry have not resolved the question of how DNA molecules can propagate life in all its forms—remaining within chemical and physical limits, while attaining an extraordinary capacity to alter the way chemical and physical laws actually manifest themselves on the surface of our planet.

Higher up the ladder of equilibrium systems, the same mystery prevails. Ideas, conveyed in signs, symbols, and messages passing from person to person, certainly affect the ecological equilibrium around us by organizing and directing human intervention in myriad natural processes. Yet external realities also impinge on ideas, even though semiotic equilibria develop a dynamic of their own, which is only loosely connected to any of the lower equilibrium systems within which they operate.

Yet, in spite of the very loose connection between our semiotic systems and the material world, human successes have been truly extraordinary. We have transformed natural landscapes beyond recognition by exporting unexpected and undesired outcomes to some sort of boundary separating field from wasteland, us from them, the managed and predictable from the rest. The "rest" is of course where catastrophe continues to lurk. Indeed, the more perfect any particular patch of ordered activity may be, the more it alters older equilibria and the greater the resulting fragility. That, at least, seems a plausible summation of our entire endeavor to control ourselves and the world around us.

Modern societies, armed with contemporary levels of science and technology, are enormously powerful. No one doubts that. Yet they are no less vulnerable. Our reliance on flow-through production and consumption creates innumerable bottlenecks, where any obstruction becomes critical if prolonged. Think of what would happen if farmers failed to plant a crop next spring because gasoline and diesel fuel no longer flowed to their tractors. What would happen to a modern city if electric current were cut off for a few days? Or, to be really up to date, consider the consequences of the erasure of computer-stored data for our banks, the internal revenue service, and our society.

It certainly seems as though every gain in precision in the coordination of human activity and every heightening of efficiency in production were matched by a new vulnerability to breakdown. If this really is the case, then the conservation of catastrophe may indeed be a law of nature like the conservation of energy.

The big bang of atomic annihilation is, I suppose, the ultimate and now fully attainable human catastrophe, even though our warheads at their worst are only a puny, pathetic echo of the big bang with which our universe is thought to have begun. Nevertheless, I do not mean to imply that colossal human tragedy masquerading as cosmic comedy is the destined end of history. On the contrary, I tend to discount such eschatological views, probably more for temperamental than for intellectual reasons. As a historian who dwells cheerfully with the past, I am moved to say that in thinking ahead we ought to bear in mind how very many times human intelligence and ingenuity have prevailed, solving one sort of problem only to create new ones, of course, but nevertheless *surviving* and transforming the face of the earth far more rapidly and radically than any other species has ever done before. With such a record, we ought not to despair but rather to rejoice in how much we human beings can do in the way of capturing energy from the world around us and bending it to our purposes and wants, intensifying the risk of catastrophe with each new success.

Notes

The Great Frontier

LECTURE I

1. Frederick Jackson Turner, *The Frontier in American History* (New York, 1920), p. 4. This book is a reprint of Turner's essays.
2. Ibid., p. 23.
3. Ibid., p. 37.
4. Ibid., p. 37.
5. Margaret Walsh, *The American Frontier Revisited* (Atlantic Highlands, N.J., 1981), summarizes recent debate; Ray Allen Billington, *The American Frontier Thesis: Attack and Defense*, rev. ed. (Washington, D.C., 1971), remains, however the best survey of the subject, offering a magistral and judicious, though firmly pious, treatment of Turnerian historiography.
6. Walter Webb, *The Great Frontier* (New York, 1952). The idea for this book dated back to 1936, and matured in graduate seminars subsequently. Cf. Necah Stewart Furman, *Walter Prescott Webb: His Life and Impact* (Albuquerque, 1976), p. 108.
7. His friends established an annual Walter Webb Memorial lecture series at the University of Texas, Arlington, from which two books relevant to my theme resulted: *Essays on Walter Prescott Webb*, The Walter Prescott Webb Memorial Lectures, X (Austin, 1976), and George Wolfskill and Stanley Palmer, eds., *Essays on Frontier History* (Austin, 1981).
8. The enterprise was analogous to Turner's effort to emancipate U.S. history from thralldom to Europe and was pursued with the same obdurate provincialism, emphasizing autochthonous traditions and denying or minimizing external, especially European, impacts and global connections.

The same climate of opinion reinforced from a quite different quarter by narrow-minded political persecution, seems to have buried Owen Lattimore's elegant essay, "The Frontier in History." This was first presented to the Tenth International Congress of the Historical Sciences in 1955, and reprinted in Owen Lattimore, *Studies in Frontier History: Collected Essays, 1928-1958* (London, 1962), pp. 469-91. Lattimore's global vision anticipates my own in interesting ways, though I read his work only after completing these lectures and found no reason to change what I had said in the light of his remarks.

9. William H. McNeill, *The Rise of the West: A History of the Human Community* (Chicago, 1963), used this hypothesis to make sense of the world's history.

10. Nevertheless, both Europe and Japan were subjugated to invaders from the steppe very early in their history, and had to repel a Mongol threat at the apex of steppe military power in the thirteenth century.

11. James Lee, Ph.D. dissertation, University of Chicago, forthcoming, provides the best analysis of the centuries-long process of Chinese expansion, but cf. also Herold J. Wiens, *China's March Towards the Tropics* (Hamden, Conn., 1954).

12. On a smaller scale other rice-paddy societies shared Chinese powers of expansion. The Japanese moved north through their islands at the expense of the Ainu, for example, in much the same fashion as the Chinese went south; and within recent centuries rice-paddy fields spread across Java from a plurality of initial lodgments, supplanting slash-and-burn cultivation. Cf. Takane Matsuo, *Rice and Rice Cultivation in Japan* (Tokyo, 1961), pp. 1-2; Geertz, *Agricultural Involution: The Process of Ecological Change in Indonesia* (Berkeley and Los Angeles, 1966), pp. 38-46.

13. This reconstruction of events is by no means universally agreed upon. Russian plague experts assume that infection of the steppe rodents was age-old, and some western scholars accept this assumption for no good reason except that Russian authorities can be cited for the opinion. Arguments for the view here set forth can be found in William H. McNeill, *Plagues and Peoples* (New York, 1976), pp. 190-96.

14. For Russian northern expansion see Raymond H. Fisher, *The Russian Fur Trade, 1550-1770* (Berkeley, 1943).

15. William H. McNeill, *Plagues and Peoples*, pp. 199-216.

16. See the impassioned but epidemiologically uninformed account in Farley Mowat, *The Desperate People* (Boston, 1959).

17. Ralph A. Austin, "From the Atlantic to the Indian Ocean: European Abolition, the African Slave Trade, and Asian Economic Structures," in David Eltis and James Walvin, eds., *The Abolition of the Atlantic Slave Trade: Origins and Effects in Europe, Africa and the Americas* (Madison, Wis., 1981), p. 136, suggests that as many as 17

million Africans entered Islamic slavery between A.D. 650 and 1920. His efforts to estimate rates of traffic, spelled out in earlier articles cited in the above, suggest that rather more than half this total left their native communities after 1500. If these estimates are anywhere near right, the numbers of Africans crossing the Atlantic and the number crossing the Sahara and the Red Sea-Indian Ocean matched one another quite closely.

18. Drastic disorganization of traditional cultural values invited self-destructive escape into alcoholism among native peoples of the frontier. Cf. Mark Twain, *Life on the Mississippi*, ch. 60, "Speculations and Conclusions": "How solemn and beautiful is the thought that the earliest pioneer of civilization, the van-leader of civilization, is never the steamboat, never the railroad, never the newspaper, never the Sabbath-school, never the missionary—but always whisky! Such is the case. Look history over: you will see. The missionary comes after the whisky—I mean he arrives after the whisky has arrived; next comes the poor immigrant, with ax and hoe and rifle; next the trader; next the miscellaneous rush; next the gambler, desperado and high-wayman, and all their kindred in sin of both sexes; and next the smart chap who has bought up an old grant that covers all the land; this brings the lawyer tribe; the vigilance committee brings the under-taker. All these interests bring the newspaper; the newspaper starts up politics and a railroad; all hands turn to and build a church and a jail—and behold! civilization is established forever in the land."

19. Stanley L. Engerman, "Servants to Slaves to Servants: Contract Labor and European Expansion" forthcoming in H. van den Boogaart and P. C. Emmer, eds., *Colonialism and Migration: Indentured Labour Before and After Slavery* (The Hague: Martinus Nijhoff/ Leiden University Press, Comparative Studies in Overseas History, Vol. VI).

20. David Eltis, "Free and Coerced Transatlantic Migrations: Some Comparisons," *American Historical Review*, forthcoming, Table 3 gives a grand total of 1,250,000 Europeans as emigrating to Brazil and Spanish America, excluding Peru, prior to 1825; but this total rests on a collocation of very flimsy estimates. Peter Boyd-Bowman, "The Regional Origins of the Earliest Spanish Colonists of America," *Modern Language Association Publications*, 71 (1956), 1152-72, calculates that 200,000 Spaniards reached America by 1600. James Lockhard, *Spanish Peru, 1532-1560* (Madison, 1968), p. 12, says that 8,000

Spaniards reached Peru within the first 25 years of the conquest. These were the only statistically careful estimates I found.

21. Engerman, *op.cit.*, p. 11. The landmark study was Philip Curtin, *The Atlantic Slave Trade: A Census* (Madison, 1969). Engerman's figure represents only minor modifications of Curtin's original calculations.

22. David W. Galenson, *White Servitude in Colonial America* (Cambridge, 1981), p. 17 and *passim*. I owe my chance to see Engerman's unpublished essay, cited above, to Professor Galenson's kindness in acting as intermediary.

23. Codfish were exceptional inasmuch as even small fishing ships could sail back to Europe at the end of the season and market their salted catch without any centralized management whatever.

24. Cf. Roger Mols, *Introduction à la démographie historique des villes d'Europe du XIVe au XVIIIe siècle*, 2 vols. (Louvain, 1955), for telling examples of the frequency and severity of local disease disasters in early modern centuries.

25. W.E.D. Allen, *The Ukraine: A History* (Cambridge, 1940), Boris Nolde, *La Formation de l'empire russe* (Paris, 1953), and William H. McNeill, *Europe's Steppe Frontier, 1500-1800* (Chicago, 1964), analyze this struggle.

LECTURE II

1. The landmark book is Emmanuel Le Roy Ladurie, *Times of Feast, Times of Famine: A History of Climate since the Year 1000* (New York, 1971).

2. No general history of the migration of American food crops exists. Berthold Laufer, *The American Plant Migration* I. *The Potato* (Chicago, 1938), projected such a work and wrote a preliminary essay on the potato before he died. With the exception of a few precocious places like Ireland, the eighteenth century was the time when the new crops became widespread—reflecting the close reciprocal relation between an enlarged labor force and increased food production.

3. This is the thesis of William H. McNeill, *Plagues and Peoples*, pp. 240-44. See also Emmanuel Le Roy Ladurie, "Un Concept: l'unification microbienne du monde (XIVe-XVIIe siècles)," *Revue suisse*

Notes

d'histoire, 23 (1973), 627-96. Michael W. Flinn, *The European Demographic System, 1500-1850* (Baltimore, 1981), offers an incisive summary of recent advances in demographic history. For what Flinn calls the eighteenth-century break-out from older equilibria, see pp. 76-101.

4. Ping-ti Ho, *Studies on the Population of China, 1368-1953* (Cambridge, Mass., 1959), p. 278.

5. Marcel R. Reinhard and André Armengaud, *Histoire générale de la population mondiale* (Paris, 1961), pp. 156, 180.

6. Reinhard and Armengaud, *op.cit.*, p. 205.

7. Robert W. Fogel and Stanley L. Engerman, *Time on the Cross: The Economics of American Negro Slavery* (Boston, 1974), pp. 25-29; Nicolas Sanchez-Albornoz, *The Population of Latin America: A History* (Berkeley and Los Angeles, 1974), pp. 86-145.

8. Clifford Geertz, *Agricultural Involution: The Process of Ecological Change in Indonesia* (Berkeley and Los Angeles, 1966), p. 99.

9. Phyllis Deane and W. A. Cole, *British Economic Growth, 1688-1959* (Cambridge, 1962), set forth the proposition authoritatively and W. A. Cole, "Eighteenth Century Economic Growth Revisited," *Explorations in Economic History* 10 (1973), pp. 327-48, reaffirmed his earlier conclusion a decade later. J. Habakkuk, *Population Growth and Economic Development since 1750* (New York, 1971), concurred.

10. On population and the French Revolution, see Oliven F. Hufton, *The Poor in Eighteenth Century France* (Oxford, 1974), and Y. LeMoigne, "Population et subsistence à Strassbourg au XVIIIe siècle" in M. Bouloisseau et al., *Contributions à l'histoire démographique de la révolution française* (Paris, 1962); W. H. McNeill, *The Pursuit of Power: Technology, Armed Force and Society since 1000* (Chicago, 1982), pp. 185-214.

11. Charles Manning Hope Clark, *A History of Australia*, 5 vols. (Melbourne, 1962-1978), is a standard authority. Cf. also H. C. Allen, *Bush and Backwoods: A Comparison of the Frontier in Australia and the United States* (Lansing, Mich., 1959).

12. Two fine books attest to recent American interest in comparison of our national frontier experience with that of South Africa: Howard Lamar and Leonard Thompson, eds., *The Frontier in History: North American and Southern African Compared* (New Haven, Conn., 1981) and George M. Frederickson, *White Supremacy: A Comparative Study in American and South African History* (New York,

1981). For a briefer but incisive analysis, cf. Leonard Thompson, "The Southern African Frontier in Comparative Perspective," in George Wolfskill and Stanley Palmer, eds., *Essays on Frontiers in World History* (Austin, Texas, 1981), pp. 86-120. For the early period, Richard Elphick and Hermann Giliomee, eds., *The Shaping of South African Society, 1652-1820* (Capetown, 1979), is especially remarkable for its ethnographic and geographical sensitivity. C. W. de Kiewit, *A History of South Africa: Social and Economic* (London, 1941), is still valuable, though Monica Wilson and Leonard Thompson, eds., *The Oxford History of South Africa*, 2 vols. (Oxford, 1969, 1971), is now a standard authority for South African history as a whole.

13. E. Bradford Burns, *A History of Brazil* (New York, 1970), pp. 42ff. Paulista *bandierantes*, Cossack hordes, and Boer commandos were strikingly similar frontier institutions. Each was constituted by a voluntary association of free men who, for a limited period of time, surrendered their ordinary liberty and submitted to military discipline under some chosen leader. Both Cossack hordes and Brazilian *bandierantes* were eventually annexed by their respective imperial governments; the Boer commandos, however, resisted any such taming by the English and instead turned against the imperial connection in 1880 and again in the Boer War of 1899-1902.

14. Hartwell Bowsfield, *Louis Riel: The Rebel and the Hero* (Toronto, 1971), tells the story.

15. The Mormons thus recapitulated the experience of the world's earliest civilizations. Religious authorities in the Tigris-Euphrates, Nile, and Indus valleys created a social hierarchy of unprecedented power and developed human skills as never before, all on a basis of irrigation agriculture that required large-scale pooling of labor for its maintenance. In exactly the same way, Brigham Young raised the Mormon community far above the level otherwise attainable by pioneers in the desert frontiers of North America. His early concentration of public resources on monumental temple-building aptly symbolizes this link with his remote predecessors, whose ziggurats and pyramids still astound us. Cf. Leonard J. Arrington, *Great Basin Kingdom: An Economic History of the Latter Day Saints, 1830-1900* (Cambridge, Mass., 1958), pp. 339-41 and *passim*.

16. On the Mennonites, see Benjamin Heinrich Unruh, *Die niederdeutschen Hintergründe der mennonitischen Ostwanderung im 16., 17. und 19. Jahrhundert* (Karlsruhe, 1955); A. H. Unruh, *Die Ge-*

schichte der Mennoniten-Brudergemeinde, 1860-1954 (Winnipeg, 1954). For Old Believers, Robert O. Crummey, *The Old Believers and the World of Anti-Christ: The Vyg Community and the Russian State, 1695-1855* (Madison, 1970), is especially informative.

17. de Kiewit, *op.cit.*, p. 76.

18. A famous work of Brazilian literature portrays this encounter, Enclides da Cunha, *Os Sertões*, translated by Samuel Putnam, ed., *Rebellion in the Backlands* (Chicago, 1944).

19. Why the United States did not abolish slavery peaceably whereas other slave-holding societies did so is an interesting question that deserves more investigation. For a recent and very persuasive analysis of why southern poor whites rallied to the slaveholders' interest as they did, see George M. Frederickson, *White Supremacy*, pp. 150-62.

20. Jerome Blum, *The End of the Old Order in Rural Europe* (Princeton, 1978), provides a magistral overview.

21. de Kiewit, *op.cit.*, pp. 88-276, gives a clear and coolly critical account of South African labor practices and race policy. Frederickson, *op.cit.*, pp. 199-238, illuminates differences between recent American and South African patterns of racial and industrial labor relations.

22. Hugh Tinker, *A New System of Slavery: The Export of Indian Labour Overseas, 1830-1920* (London, 1974), provides a detailed picture of how Indian coolie labor was recruited, exported, maltreated, and shipped back to India. Tinker's approach is descriptive and moral rather than statistical.

23. Statistics for Indian indentured labor come from Kingsley Davis, *The Population of India and Pakistan* (Princeton, 1951), pp. 99, 115-20. On indentured labor as a substitute for slavery see Stanley L. Engerman, "Servants to Slaves to Servants: Contract Labor and European Expansion," forthcoming in E. van den Boogaart and P. C. Emmer, eds., *Colonialism and Migration: Indentured Labour Before and After Slavery* (The Hague: Martinus Nijhoff/Leiden University Press, Comparative Studies in Overseas History, Vol. VI). I owe my understanding of the matter to this paper.

24. The figure of 46.2 million comes from Engerman, *op.cit.*, that for Russian colonization from Donald W. Treadgold, *The Great Siberian Migration* (Princeton, 1957), pp. 33-35.

25. The south, nevertheless, invented legal forms of labor contracts that preserved a good deal of compulsion for Blacks after 1863. See

Notes

William Cohen, "Negro Involuntary Servitude in the South, 1865-1940: A Preliminary Analysis," *Journal of Southern History* 42 (1976), 31-60.

26. Market exposure closely resembles disease exposure. Initial intrusion of civilized diseases upon a previously isolated community is always disastrous; similarly, market relations initially destroy local subsistence economies and traditional ways of life. Sporadic exposure remains costly too. For diseases, this means periodic epidemic with sudden, severe, and unpredictable die-off of young and old; for market relations it provokes the acute frictions between buyer and seller that characterized frontier life and upon which I have put considerable emphasis in these lectures. But, in both instances, fuller and more continuous contacts diminish costs. Endemic infection concentrates disease deaths among easily replaced infants even if lethality is not diminished, as usually also occurs; and full exposure to market options allows suitably conditioned individuals to profit from alternative opportunities by choosing shrewdly what to do and with whom to make contracts. The economic equivalent of infant die-off also exists among those who, for whatever reason, remain incompetent in a market environment, making wrong choices and offering themselves as victims for more calculating and ruthless individuals. The history of civilization could, perhaps, be written around the way exchanges among human beings have altered through time in response to evolving patterns of transport and communication that always disseminated potent disease germs and no less potent goods and services, and did so in ever-changing ways.

27. Alfred Chandler, *The Visible Hand: The Managerial Revolution in America* (Cambridge, Mass., 1977), has instructive things to say about the development of corporate management since 1880.

28. Cf. the critique of Turner's ambivalence between the values of "civilization" and "cultural primitivism," in Henry Nash Smith, *Virgin Land: The American West as Symbol and Myth* (Cambridge, Mass., 1950), Ch. 22.

The Human Condition

MICROPARASITISM, MACROPARASITISM, AND THE URBAN TRANSMUTATION

1. How powerful such natural microparasites could be in limiting human life is evidenced by the survival into the twentieth century of big game animals in east Africa in those landscapes where tsetse flies infect cattle and human intruders with lethal sleeping sickness. Malaria also put similar, if somewhat less drastic, limitations on human life in Africa until very recently.

2. This interpretation of Pleistocene die-offs is not universally accepted. Climatic changes incident to the most recent advance and withdrawal of the northern ice sheet may have mattered more. Human dispersal coincided with sharp climatic change, and it is a mistake to try to separate the influence of the one from that of the other in upsetting older ecological balances.

3. William H. McNeill, *Plagues and Peoples* (New York, 1976).

4. The best introduction to this theme that I am acquainted with is Frank Fenner and F. N. Ratcliffe, *Myxomatosis* (Cambridge: Cambridge University Press, 1965). This book describes in detail the way in which rabbit populations of Australia and Europe reacted to their encounter with a new and, to begin with, enormously lethal infection that had been deliberately introduced by human agents in hope of thereby reducing rabbit densities. Adaptation by the myxomatosis virus due to selective survival of less lethal strains and adaptation among rabbits for survival in face of the new infection combined to stabilize rabbit populations (at a much lower level than before) after about three years had passed.

MICROPARASITISM, MACROPARASITISM, AND THE COMMERCIAL TRANSMUTATION

1. William H. McNeill, *Plagues and Peoples* (New York, 1976).

Index